50 American Women of Courage & Vision

by
Susan E. Edgar
and
Kathleen J. Edgar

PHOTO CREDITS

AP/Wide World: pp. 12, 17, 23, 40, 57, 67, 70, 74, 86, 92, 98, 108, 114, 126, 154, 165, 171, 174, 183, 185, 189, 194, 197, 205, 211, 222, 238, 278, 284, 287 • **The Granger Collection:** pp. 47, 51, 120, 132, 142, 228, 256, 262, 273 • **Rachel Carson History Project:** p. 62 • **Library of Congress, Prints and Photography Division:** pp. 80, 160, 244, 268 • **NASA:** p. 177 • **Archive Photos:** p. 233

Copyright © 2007 Kidsbooks, LLC
www.kidsbooks.com®

Reading Challenge® is an imprint of Kidsbooks, LLC

All rights reserved including the right
of reproduction in whole or in part in any form.

Manufactured in China

1206-1C

Visit us at **www.readingchallenge.com**

Contents

Introduction 5
Jane Addams: *Social Reformer and World Peace Activist* ... 6
Marian Anderson: *Singer and Diplomat* 11
Susan B. Anthony: *Women's Rights Leader* 16
Mary Kay Ash: *Entrepreneur* 22
Clara Barton: *Founder of the American Red Cross* 28
Daisy Bates: *Civil-rights Activist* 33
Mary McLeod Bethune: *Educator* 39
Elizabeth Blackwell: *First Female Doctor* 45
Nellie Bly: *Journalist* 50
Margaret Bourke-White: *Photojournalist* 56
Rachel Carson: *Biologist and Environmentalist* 61
Amelia Earhart: *Pioneering Pilot* 67
Dian Fossey: *Zoologist* 73
Betty Friedan: *Founder of the Feminist Movement* 79
Althea Gibson: *Tennis Champion* 85
Katharine Graham: *Publisher* 91
Martha Graham: *Founder of Modern Dance* 97
Ella Grasso: *First Female Governor in the U.S.* 102
Fannie Lou Hamer: *Civil-rights Activist* 107
Audrey Hepburn: *Actor and Humanitarian* 113
Anne Hutchinson: *Champion of Religious Freedom* 119
Mae Jemison: *Doctor, Engineer, Astronaut* 125
Mother Jones: *Labor Leader* 131
Helen Keller: *Activist for the Disabled* 136

Billie Jean King: *Tennis Champion* **141**
Maggie Kuhn: *Advocate for the Elderly* **147**
Maya Lin: *Architect and Artist* **153**
Belva Lockwood: *Lawyer and Women's Rights Activist* .. **159**
Margaret Mead: *Anthropologist* **164**
Toni Morrison: *Author and Teacher* **170**
Ellen Ochoa: *First Hispanic American Woman in Space* .. **176**
Sandra Day O'Connor: *U.S. Supreme Court Justice* **182**
Georgia O'Keeffe: *Painter* **188**
Rosa Parks: *Civil-rights Activist* **193**
Jeannette Rankin: *First Woman Elected to Congress* ... **199**
Janet Reno: *Attorney General of the U.S.* **204**
Sally Ride: *First American Woman in Space* **210**
Eleanor Roosevelt: *Social Reformer and First Lady* ... **215**
Wilma Rudolph: *Track-and-Field Star* **221**
Sacagawea: *Interpreter and Explorer* **226**
Elizabeth Cady Stanton: *Women's Rights Leader* **232**
Gloria Steinem: *Journalist and Feminist* **237**
Ida M. Tarbell: *Investigative Reporter* **243**
Sojourner Truth: *Crusader for African American Rights* . **249**
Harriet Tubman: *Conductor on the*
    Underground Railroad **255**
Mary Edwards Walker: *Army Doctor* **261**
Ida B. Wells-Barnett: *Antilynching Crusader* **267**
Laura Ingalls Wilder: *Author* **272**
Oprah Winfrey: *Talk-show Host, Actor, Humanitarian* .. **277**
Babe Didrikson Zaharias: *Athlete* **283**

Introduction

Actions speak louder than words, and role models speak volumes on values. In these short biographies, 50 American women put their courage, vision, and other important values into action. These inspiring figures faced challenges, overcame adversity, and often accomplished what no person, man or woman, had ever done before.

Harriet Tubman was determined to escape from her life as a slave, and to help other slaves escape as well. She risked her life again and again because she knew that what she was doing was right.

As one of the world's first female pilots, Amelia Earhart demonstrated to a generation of women that they are every bit as capable as men. Through her courage and adventurous spirit, she overcame the stereotypes and boundaries created by society.

When Sandra Day O'Connor could not get work at a law firm because of her gender, she started a firm of her own. She went on to become the first woman appointed to the U.S. Supreme Court, proving to the nation that gender does not determine a person's value.

Role models inspire us to aim high, do our best, and try again and again when we fail. A library of life's lessons, this collection of biographies will introduce young readers to people from whom they can learn and whose values they can respect.

Jane Addams
Social Reformer and World Peace Activist
(born 1860 • died 1935)

During the late 1800s, hundreds of thousands of immigrants from Europe and Asia came to America's shores. As the population of the U.S. increased, jobs became scarce, leaving many of the newcomers poor and homeless. In response, Jane Addams worked to help the poor make better lives for themselves. She was a pioneer of the social reform movement and urged society to change for the better.

A Social Reformer Is Born

Born on September 6, 1860, in Cedarville, Illinois, Jane was one of nine children. Her father was a state senator and a friend of President Abraham Lincoln.

Jane attended Rockford Female Seminary and Women's Medical College, but she was unsure of what she wanted to do with her life. When she was 27, Jane Addams traveled to Europe with her friend Ellen Starr.

Jane Addams

While in England, she visited Toynbee Hall, a settlement house in London. Settlement houses offered cultural and educational programs to poor families in an effort to bring new life to communities. Addams and Starr were impressed by this idea and returned home with plans to create a settlement house in Chicago.

Hull House

First, Jane Addams and Ellen Starr purchased the Hull estate, a large, run-down mansion in a poor section of Chicago. After making some repairs, the two women opened Hull House in 1889. Modeled after Toynbee Hall in London, Hull House helped needy families. It also offered educational programs for immigrants, and day care for the children of working parents.

> "Private beneficence is totally inadequate to deal with the vast numbers of the city's disinherited."
> —Jane Addams

During the next several years, 12 more buildings were added, making Hull House one of the largest centers of its kind in the United States. Private citizens and other charity groups donated funds to keep the settlement growing. Hull House also offered training programs for people who wanted jobs as social workers.

Following the success of Hull House, Addams turned her talents to social and labor issues. Speaking out on topics such as public education, labor reform, and the rights of immigrants, Addams worked to create laws to help average people. These laws included limiting work to eight hours each day, providing wages to workers who got hurt on the job, and making sure factories were safe.

Pleading for Peace

In 1914, World War I broke out in Europe. Addams believed that people should live peacefully and not harm each other. In 1915, she traveled to the Netherlands to join more than 1,000 women from Europe and North America to discuss putting an end to the war. Known as the International Congress of Women, the group wanted to meet with government officials from the warring nations in "protest against the madness and horror of war." Addams was elected president of the Congress.

The Congress chose 30 women to travel throughout Europe. As president of the group, Addams represented women who had lost loved ones in the war. The group insisted that average citizens and prisoners of war be treated fairly. They also suggested that a Society of Nations be established to act as a worldwide

---

TOPICAL TIDBIT

The United Nations

The United Nations (UN) is an international organization dedicated to maintaining peace throughout the world. Based on a proposal drafted by the International Congress of Women in 1915, the United Nations Charter was signed by representatives from 51 nations on June 26, 1945, in San Francisco, California. (A charter is an official document that creates an organization and spells out its rules and regulations.)

governing body. World War I lasted until November 1918, but government officials did adopt many of the ideas presented by the International Congress of Women—especially those regarding the treatment of prisoners of war.

After the war, Addams kept working for reforms. In 1920, she helped found the American Civil Liberties Union (ACLU), which is still active today. In 1931, she was awarded the Nobel Peace Prize for her efforts in social work and in pleading for peace throughout the world.

Worthy of Remembrance

Jane Addams died on May 21, 1935, in Chicago. Hull House, now a museum, remains as a monument to Addams, one of the greatest social reformers in U.S. history.

LIFE EVENTS

1860
Jane Addams is born in Cedarville, Illinois.

1889
Impressed with a successful settlement house in London, Addams and her friend Ellen Starr open Hull House in Chicago.

1910
Addams's autobiography, entitled *Twenty Years at Hull House*, is published.

1919-1935
Addams helps found, and serves as president of, the Women's International League for Peace and Freedom.

1931
Addams is awarded the Nobel Peace Prize in recognition of her efforts in social work and reform.

Marian Anderson
Singer and Diplomat
(born 1897 • died 1993)

When Marian Anderson was a little girl, she displayed an incredible talent for singing. People who heard her perform knew that she would be famous one day. As an African American woman, she faced many obstacles. To escape the rampant racism in the U.S., Anderson decided to perform in Europe. She became a success abroad long before her talents were recognized in her own country.

The Gift of Voice

Marian Anderson was born on February 27, 1897, in Philadelphia, Pennsylvania. (Some records list her birth year as 1902.) Her parents had little money, so Marian helped out by doing odd jobs, such as scrubbing floors. The family could not afford singing lessons, so Marian joined her church choir.

In time, friends, family, and church members realized that Marian was a gifted singer. They raised money to send her to music school. The music

Marian Anderson prepares to sing on the steps of the Lincoln Memorial, April 9, 1939.

school, however, was segregated, and would not admit Marian because she was black. Marian's voice would not be silenced. She used the money for singing lessons.

Marian Anderson's big break came in 1925 when she won a talent contest. She was 28 years old. The prize was to sing in a concert with the famous New York Philharmonic Orchestra.

Prejudice at Home

In America of the 1930s, people were denied things based on their gender and race. African Americans were refused service in restaurants and denied jobs. As an African American woman, Anderson faced prejudice every day. And her career was affected because she was only allowed to perform in black concert halls in the United States. Other venues were strictly off-limits to her.

In Europe, there were fewer restrictions for blacks. Anderson first performed in Europe in 1930, and gave many concerts there during the next five years. She attracted a huge following and received several scholarships to continue her education in Europe.

> "As long as you keep a person down, some part of you has to be down there to hold him down, so it means you cannot soar as you otherwise might."
> —Marian Anderson

In 1935, Anderson returned to the U.S. to make her official New York concert debut. Four years later, she wanted to perform at Constitutional Hall in Washington D.C. When she tried to book the hall, however, she was turned away because she was black.

Constitution Hall was owned by the Daughters of the American Revolution (DAR)—an organization of prominent women who were descendants of the country's founding fathers. The group had not allowed African Americans to perform at the hall since 1932.

Marian Anderson Shines Through

One of the most famous members of the DAR was First Lady Eleanor Roosevelt. When Roosevelt found out why Anderson could not rent the hall, she was outraged, and resigned from the DAR in protest. Many other DAR members did, too. The White House made arrangements for Anderson to sing at the Lincoln Memorial instead, and about 75,000 people went to hear the concert.

As Anderson sang that day, it was obvious that thousands of people in the U.S. supported her remarkable talent. In her autobiography, *My Lord, What a Morning*, she remembered how she felt during that concert. "I had a feeling that a great wave of goodwill

TOPICAL TIDBIT

Contra What?

Marian Anderson was among the best contraltos ever heard. A *contralto* is a singer who can hit a wide range of notes. Anderson could sing lower tenor parts and higher mezzo (mid) soprano parts. As a result, she could perform many types of music.

poured out from these people."

Anderson again made headlines in 1955, when she became the first black performer to sing with the Metropolitan Opera. Several years later, she expanded her career to include diplomatic work: In 1958, she was appointed as a delegate to the United Nations. Shortly before her death on April 8, 1993, Anderson was honored with a Grammy Award for Lifetime Achievement.

A World-renowned Voice

Marian Anderson overcame prejudice to become a world-renowned singer. Her voice won over audiences throughout the world. She received many awards, including the Presidential Medal of Freedom, which she received in 1963 from President Lyndon B. Johnson. In 1973, she was inducted into the National Women's Hall of Fame.

LIFE EVENTS

1897
Marian Anderson is born in Philadelphia, Pennsylvania.

1939
Denied the right to sing at Constitution Hall in Washington, D.C., Anderson sings at the Lincoln Memorial.

1955
Anderson makes her debut at the New York Metropolitan Opera House.

1956
Anderson publishes her autobiography, *My Lord, What a Morning*.

1984
Anderson is the first recipient of New York City's Human Rights Award.

1993
Marian Anderson dies.

Susan B. Anthony
Women's Rights Leader
(born 1820 • died 1906)

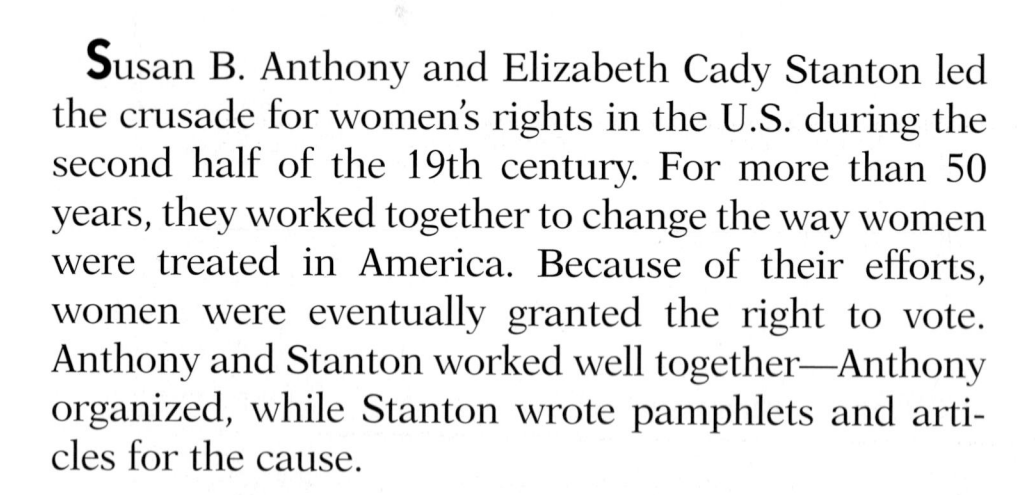

Susan B. Anthony and Elizabeth Cady Stanton led the crusade for women's rights in the U.S. during the second half of the 19th century. For more than 50 years, they worked together to change the way women were treated in America. Because of their efforts, women were eventually granted the right to vote. Anthony and Stanton worked well together—Anthony organized, while Stanton wrote pamphlets and articles for the cause.

Fighting for the Cause

Susan Brownell Anthony was born on February 15, 1820, in Adams, Massachusetts. She was one of eight children. Susan's father, the owner of a cotton mill, encouraged his children to get a good education. Susan was a bright child who learned to read and write when she was just three years old. She did very well in school and became a teacher when she was only 15.

◇ Susan B. Anthony ◇

Susan B. Anthony had strong ideas about the way people should treat one another. She was an abolitionist—someone who believed that slavery should be outlawed. She believed that all people should be treated equally and fairly, and that no one had the right to own another person. She then became active in the temperance movement, which was designed to stamp out drunkenness and the use of alcohol. She also became involved in the women's rights movement.

The Revolution

In 1850, Susan B. Anthony met Elizabeth Cady Stanton, one of the founders of the women's rights movement. The two women became instant friends, as both had the same ideas: Slavery and liquor were wrong and should be abolished. However, they believed that their views on alcohol and slavery would not be taken seriously while the laws in the U.S. treated women as second-class citizens. They both agreed that there was only one way to influence people to their way of thinking—to become voting citizens. Anthony and Stanton united themselves to the cause of women's suffrage—the right to vote.

> "Men, their rights and nothing more; women, their rights and nothing less."
> —Susan B. Anthony

For the next 50 years, the two women devoted their time and energy to that cause. In the late 1860s, they formed the National Woman Suffrage Association (NWSA) and published *The Revolution*, a newspaper dedicated to women's voting issues.

Jailed for Freedom

In 1872 Anthony broke the law by voting in the presidential election. She went to the polls in her hometown of Rochester, New York, along with 12 of her supporters. The women persuaded the election inspectors to let them vote. Two weeks later, all of them—the women and the inspectors—were arrested and put on trial. During the trial, the judge feared that the jury might let the women go, so he dismissed the jury and found Anthony guilty. She refused to pay the fine of $100, but the judge let the case drop. The inspectors were also fined, although none of the other women were.

For many years after, Anthony traveled across the country, inviting men and women to join the suffrage movement. She gave speeches on street corners and in lecture halls about a woman's right to vote. Anthony was not a dynamic public speaker. However,

---

TOPICAL TIDBIT

Not for Ourselves Alone

In the late 1990s, filmmakers and historians Ken Burns and Geoffrey C. Ward chronicled the history of the women's suffrage movement in a documentary film and book, *Not for Ourselves Alone: The Story of Elizabeth Cady Stanton and Susan B. Anthony*.

the words in the speeches, written by Elizabeth Cady Stanton, still had a great impact on her audiences.

In 1878, Anthony appeared before the U.S. Congress and proposed an amendment, or change, to the U.S. Constitution. Written by Stanton, the amendment called for the government to grant women the right to vote. The amendment failed, but that did not stop Anthony. She appeared before Congress each year until her death, hoping that the amendment would someday pass.

Lasting Influence

When Susan B. Anthony died on March 13, 1906, in Rochester, New York, the amendment had not become law. Other suffragists followed in Anthony's place, however, and, in 1920, the states approved the 19th Amendment to the U.S. Constitution,

LIFE EVENTS

1820
Susan Brownell Anthony is born in Adams, Massachusetts.

1868-1870
Anthony works as the editor of the feminist weekly, *Revolution*.

1869
Anthony and Elizabeth Cady Stanton found the National Woman Suffrage Association.

1872
Anthony illegally votes in the presidential election. She is arrested for civil disobedience, but the case is dropped.

1906
Anthony dies in Rochester, New York.

1920
U.S. women are granted the right to vote.

granting women the right to vote. Later that year, more than eight million women voted for the first time under what became known as the "Susan B. Anthony Amendment." In 1973, she was inducted into the National Women's Hall of Fame. In 1979, the U.S. Mint honored her by issuing the one-dollar Susan B. Anthony coin—the first U.S. currency with a woman's picture on it.

Mary Kay Ash
Entrepreneur
(born 1918 • died 2001)

Mary Kay Ash built a costmetics empire that is still going strong today. With a sales force of more than 1.5 million people, mostly women, Mary Kay Inc. sells its products in 30 countries throughout the world. Mary Kay's business philosophy is based on the Golden Rule—Treat people as you want to be treated, and you will succeed.

"You Can Do It"

Mary Kathlyn Wagner was born in Hot Wells, Texas, on May 12, 1918. Mary Kay, as she was called, learned at an early age the value of working hard to achieve goals. When Mary Kay was a young girl, her father was diagnosed with tuberculosis (TB), a disease of the lungs. Her mother supported the family by working 14-hour days at a Houston restaurant. Mary Kay took care of her father. She also took care of preparing meals, cleaning the house, and doing other chores.

◇ Mary Kay Ash ◇

At school, Mary Kay took typing classes, always bringing home a very good report card. She joined the debate team and excelled at selling tickets for school activities. Mary Kay's mother encouraged her at every step, telling her "You can do it."

By the time she was 21, Mary Kay joined the sales force at Stanley Home Products. The company was one of the first to use the idea of in-home shopping. The way in-home shopping worked was that a homemaker would have a party, inviting her neighbors and friends. A Stanley sales associate would attend the party to show the products and how they could be used.

Mary Kay was a natural when it came to selling Stanley's product line. The line consisted of cleaning products, such as mops, brooms, and furniture polish. Mary Kay left Stanley Home Products in 1952, having won many sales awards for her efforts. She began working at World Gift Co. where she eventually made her way up the corporate ladder to national sales director. However, in 1963, Mary Kay decided she had had enough. Too many times, the management of World Gift Co. had promoted men above her—men that she had trained. And to top it off, she was earning only half the salary of what they were being paid. It wasn't fair.

TOPICAL TIDBIT

Coco Chanel

At the turn of the 20th century, women wore very restrictive clothing, such as corsets and long skirts that didn't allow them to move with ease or comfort. That all changed with new fashions created by Coco Chanel (1883–1971), a French dress designer. Coco opened a hat shop in 1913 and began designing sweaters and suits. In a bold move, she began designing slacks for women—this was unthinkable at the time. Soon, women began to wear slacks because they were comfortable and much more practical than the long skirts of the day. By the 1930s, Chanel Industries included a fashion design house, a jewelry shop, and a perfume laboratory. The most popular fragrance was Chanel No. 5, first produced in 1922 and still worn by women today.

Once Mary Kay retired from World Gift Co. in 1963, she started to write a book for women on how to achieve results in the workplace. In her notes, she modeled her "dream company"—a company that sold quality products, treated its employees fairly, and empowered women to achieve success. She began to wonder why she wasn't pursuing her dreams. She remembered her mother's words: "You can do it."

> "If you think you can, you can. And if you think you can't, you're right."
> —Mary Kay Ash

More Than Pink Cadillacs

It didn't take Mary Kay very long to make her dream company a reality. She gathered up her life savings of $5,000 and bought a formula for a quality skin care product. With the help of her husband, children, and some friends, Mary Kay Cosmetics (later called Mary Kay Inc.) opened its doors on September 13, 1963. In the first year, the company had sales of nearly $200,000. By 2004, Mary Kay Inc. boasted sales of more than $1.8 billion!

Since the company's founding, incentives have been awarded to the top sales achievers—things like diamond jewelry and furs. The ultimate prize is a pink Coupe DeVilles Cadillac, the trademark of a top Mary Kay sales director. Since 1969, the company has awarded more than 10,000 Cadillacs.

But Mary Kay Inc. is about more than just sales incentives. *Forbes* magazine listed Mary Kay Inc. as one of the "100 Best Companies to Work for in America." And for good reason: The founding principles of Mary Kay Inc. are to sell quality products and to create career opportunities for women. As Independent Beauty Consultants, each salesperson, women and men alike, choose their own schedule. Each associate works as little or as often as she or he desires. The company also offers opportunities for women to own their own business as part of the Mary Kay family.

Life After Retirement

Mary Kay retired in 1987, handing over the company's operations to her son, Richard Rogers. She wrote a number of books, including the 1995 bestseller *Mary Kay: You Can Have It All*. But, through all of her success, Mary Kay Ash wanted to do more.

In 1996, she established the Mary Kay Ash Charitable Foundation in Dallas, Texas. The foundation supports medical research for diseases that affect women, such as breast and ovarian cancer. In addition to medical research, the foundation supports programs to end violence against women. In 2005, PBS aired *Breaking the Silence: Children's Stories*, a documentary about the effects of violence and domestic abuse on women and children. The show was sponsored by the Mary Kay Ash Charitable Foundation and appeared on more than 235 stations.

A Place in History

Mary Kay Ash died November 22, 2001 in Dallas, Texas. The success of Mary Kay Inc. is a tribute to the woman who founded the company. At a time when there were few opportunities for women in the business world, Mary Kay Ash took the challenge and made it profitable. Her vision and courage serve as a model to women and girls throughout the world.

In 1999, Lifetime Television named Mary Kay Ash the Most Outstanding Woman in Business in the 20th Century.

LIFE EVENTS

1918
Mary Kay Wagner is born in Texas.

1963
Mary Kay establishes Mary Kay Cosmetics.

1965
Sales for Mary Kay Inc. exceed $1 million.

1996
Ash establishes the Mary Kay Ash Charitable Foundation.

1999
Ash is named as Lifetime's Most Outstanding Woman in Business in the 20th Century.

2001
Mary Kay Ash dies in Dallas, Texas.

2005
Mary Kay Inc. donates more than $1 million to Hurricane Katrina relief efforts.

Clara Barton
Founder of the American Red Cross
(born 1821 • died 1912)

Clara Barton devoted her life to helping others—both on the battlefield and in hospitals. She started the American Association of the Red Cross (now the American Red Cross), a relief organization that continues to provide supplies, medicine, food, and funds to people who are victims of war, natural disasters, disease epidemics, and famines.

Independent Spirit

Born Clarissa Harlowe Barton on December 25, 1821, in Oxford, Massachusetts, Clara was taught at home by her brothers and sisters, who were much older than she. She gained nursing experience by caring for one of her brothers who was ill. When Clara was 15, she became a teacher.

In 1852, Clara Barton started her own school in Bordentown, New Jersey. Under her leadership, the number of students at the school rose significantly.

Clara Barton

However, town officials told Barton that the school had become too big to be managed by a woman—a man would have to run it. In that era, people had limited ideas about what a woman could and could not do. As a result, Barton resigned.

Before the Civil War began in 1861, Barton worked as a clerk in the U.S. Patent Office. It was unusual for "proper" women to work outside the home, but Barton got away with it because she was not married. When the Civil War broke out, Barton left the Patent Office to help wounded Union soldiers.

Relief Agent

Barton raised money to provide relief (food and medical supplies) for the soldiers on the battlefield, in camps, and in hospitals. She served as a nurse, assisting surgeons who had to remove bullets, stitch up wounds, or amputate soldiers' arms and legs. She worked endless hours to help the men, earning the nickname "Angel of the Battlefield."

After the war ended in 1865, Barton tried to locate soldiers who were missing in action. In 1869, she headed to Europe to rest. While in Europe, she learned of the activities of the International Red Cross, an organization that had been formed in Switzerland in 1864.

Barton volunteered at the International Red Cross to help soldiers who were wounded in the Franco-Prussian War (1870-1871). However, the organization would not let her treat war victims because she was a woman. So Barton worked independently. She returned to the United States in 1873 and urged the country to begin its own branch of the Red Cross organization.

> "I may be compelled to face danger, but never fear it, and while our soldiers can stand and fight, I can stand and feed and nurse them."
> —Clara Barton

American Association of the Red Cross

Although the Red Cross provided many important services, the U.S. government was not interested in starting such an organization. Government officials wanted to stay out of Europe's wars and problems, and they considered the Red Cross to be a European organization. Barton worked long and hard to convince leaders to start the American Association of the Red Cross (now called the American Red Cross).

She finally succeeded in 1881 and began the American branch of the Red Cross. Barton thought that the Red Cross organizations should provide relief services to people during *all* times—in peace and war. So she urged the International Red Cross to adopt what is called the "American Amendment." It called for the organization to help victims of natural disasters and food shortages as well.

TOPICAL TIDBIT

The International Red Cross

The idea for the International Red Cross came from Henri Dunant, a Swiss humanitarian, who saw wounded soldiers left to die during the Battle of Solferino, in Italy, in 1859. In 1864, delegates from 16 countries attended a meeting in Switzerland, called the Geneva Convention, and founded the organization to help the wounded.

Serving as head of the American branch, Barton directed relief activities during the Spanish-American War, in 1898. She also oversaw assistance to victims of disasters, such as the 1889 flood in Johnstown, Pennsylvania, and the 1900 hurricane that nearly wiped out Galveston, Texas.

Despite her hard work, Barton had trouble directing others. She wanted to do things herself or in her own way. Barton was asked to resign in 1904. She died on April 12, 1912, in Glen Echo, Maryland.

Barton's Legacy

The American Red Cross has helped millions of people since 1881. It is a fitting tribute to its founder, who worked selflessly to relieve the suffering of the sick, wounded, and homeless. Her house and office in Glen Echo, Maryland, are now designated a national historic site.

LIFE EVENTS

1821
Clarissa Harlowe Barton is born in Oxford, Massachusetts.

1862
Barton serves as a front-line nurse for the Army of the Potomac.

1864
Barton serves as superintendent of nurses for the Army of the James. The same year, in Europe, the International Red Cross is founded.

1869
Barton serves in Europe during the Franco-Prussian War.

1881
Barton founds the American Red Cross. She serves as its president until 1904.

1912
Barton dies in Glen Echo, Maryland.

Daisy Bates
Civil-rights Activist
(born 1914 • died 1999)

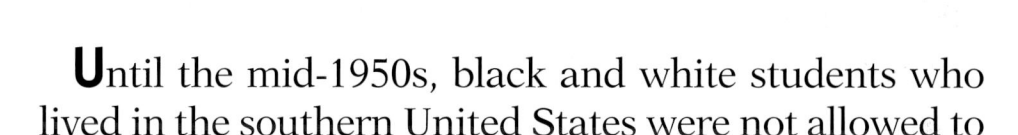

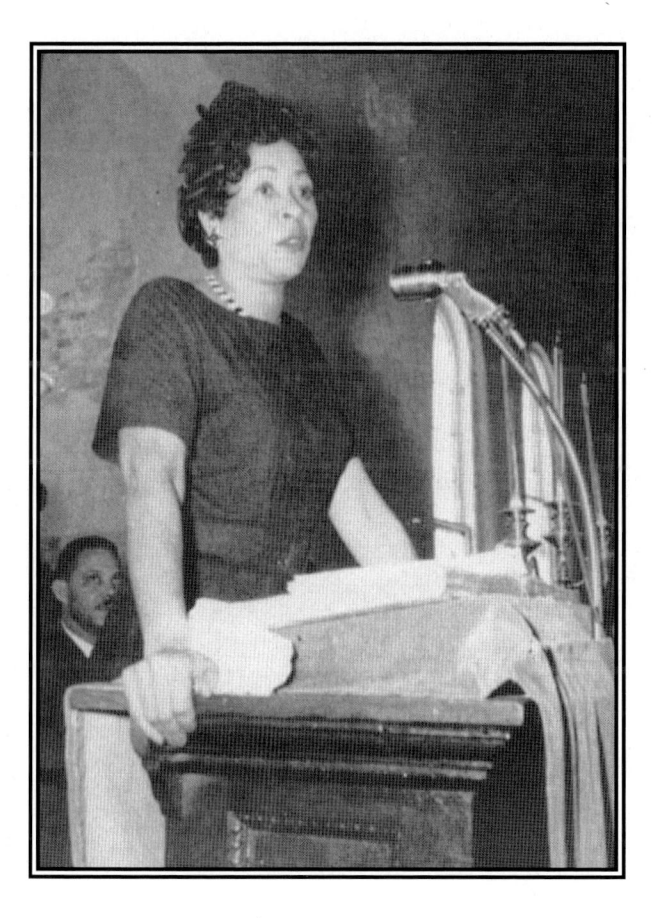

Until the mid-1950s, black and white students who lived in the southern United States were not allowed to go to the same schools. Schools for whites usually had enough books and other supplies, well-trained teachers, and free bus transportation, but schools for blacks rarely had these things. Daisy Bates not only saw this as unfair, she worked hard to help bring about change. Her efforts in the civil-rights movement made it possible for all children in the United States to receive an equal education, regardless of the color of their skin.

Overcoming Hardships

Daisy Lee Gatson was born in the small town of Huttig, Arkansas, in 1914. She never knew her biological parents. When Daisy was very young, her mother was murdered by three white men, and her father, afraid to bring charges against the murderers, left town and never returned. Daisy was adopted by friends of her parents.

Like other black children in the South, Daisy attended a segregated school. The black school was in poor condition, and the students had to use old, outdated books that the white school had thrown away.

> "Events in history occur when the time has ripened for them, but they need a spark. Little Rock was that spark at that stage of the struggle of the American Negro for justice."
> —Daisy Bates

In 1941, Daisy married Lucius Bates and moved with him to Little Rock, the capital of Arkansas. Together, they started a newspaper called the *Arkansas*

State Press, which they dedicated to helping change conditions for black people. One of their most important victories was a series of articles that showed how white police officers abused local black residents. The articles helped sway public opinion, and black officers were soon hired to patrol black neighborhoods.

The Little Rock Nine

In 1954, the U.S. Supreme Court made an historic ruling in a case known as *Brown v. Board of Education of Topeka, Kansas*. The Court ruled that, under the U.S. Constitution, segregation (separating by race) in public schools was against the law. At that time, Daisy Bates was president of the state conference of the National Association for the Advancement of Colored People (NAACP). She and other NAACP members believed that Little Rock should integrate (mix races in) its schools right away, but the city put off making any changes.

Bates knew that it was up to people like her to take action. She began escorting black students to white schools, accompanied by newspaper photographers who would capture on film the black students being turned away. Meanwhile, the NAACP was in court, seeking to force white schools to obey the ruling to integrate. Finally, after a long legal battle, a judge said that Little Rock would have to start integrating its schools in September 1957.

Nine black students agreed to attend Little Rock's Central High School. The students and their families knew that many white people in Little Rock would fight any attempt to admit them. Daisy Bates promised to protect the students against any violence—but nobody really knew what would happen.

On September 22, a rock was thrown through the front window of Bates's home, but she did not let that stop her efforts. Instead, she asked several ministers to join her in accompanying the students into the school.

On September 23, Bates and eight of the nine students gathered outside Bates's home and headed for Central High. A crowd of angry whites was milling around outside the school. While a group of white thugs were beating up four black journalists whom

TOPICAL TIDBIT

Breaking Past Barriers

The story of the Little Rock Nine was mirrored by other school-door dramas around the country. In 1962, James Meredith, a young black Air Force veteran, braved tear gas as well as an angry mob to enter the all-white University of Mississippi. In 1963, Alabama Governor George Wallace joined the guardsmen he had ordered to block the first black students trying to enter the University of Alabama. In these and other such cases, federal troops had to be sent to finally enforce the law.

they had mistaken for students, Bates and the eight real students managed to slip into school.

Meanwhile, the ninth student, Elizabeth Eckford, was on her own. Eckford, who did not have a telephone, had not heard about the plan to meet at Daisy Bates's house. When Eckford arrived at Central High, she was screamed at and spat upon by the angry mob. The girl was not harmed: Two whites stepped forward and helped her escape. She made it home safely.

The crowd of whites outside Central High would not calm down and go home. Finally, the mayor of Little Rock had the eight black students removed from the school under police protection

Because of the threat of violence, President Dwight D. Eisenhower sent army troops to the school to enforce the integration law. On September 25, Bates successfully escorted the "Little Rock Nine" into Central High. She continued to help them throughout their time at the school—even though the Little Rock police arrested her on phony charges.

A Life's Work

Daisy Bates did not stop fighting segregation. After the Little Rock Nine succeeded in desegregating the Little Rock schools, Bates spent the rest of her life campaigning for equal treatment for African Americans, trying to improve their education, and helping them register to vote.

Daisy Bates died in 1999. A few days after her death, the Little Rock Nine received Congressional Gold Medals from President Bill Clinton. At the awards ceremony, the President said of Daisy Bates: "I ask you all to remember her today, her smiling self, for that gave a lot of confidence to those whom we honor." He and other speakers that day remembered and gave tribute to Daisy Bates for her courage and hard work in winning equal treatment for all.

LIFE EVENTS

1914
Daisy Lee Gatson is born in Huttig, Arkansas.

1941
She marries Lucius Bates. In Little Rock, they start the *Arkansas State Press*, a newspaper that crusades for African American rights.

1954
The U.S. Supreme Court rules that segregated schools are unconstitutional.

1957
Daisy Bates leads nine black students integrating Little Rock's Central High School. A tense standoff with the governor gets nationwide attention.

1962
The Long Shadow of Little Rock, Bates's autobiography, is published.

Mary McLeod Bethune
Educator
(born 1875 • died 1955)

Mary McLeod Bethune devoted her life to the education and fair treatment of African Americans in the U.S. She believed that, through education, people could create better lives for themselves. Bethune worked tirelessly and rose through the ranks to become an adviser to President Franklin Roosevelt. She went on to become the first African American woman to head a federal agency.

Helping Those at Home

Mary Jane McLeod was born on July 10, 1875, on a farm near Mayesville, South Carolina. Mary's parents, Samuel and Patsy McLeod, had been slaves before gaining their freedom after the Civil War (1861-1865). Many of the McLeods' 17 children had been sold into slavery, but not Mary—she was born after her parents were free.

President Harry S. Truman with Mary McLeod Bethune, May 18, 1949.

As a young girl, Mary helped her parents on the farm, planting and harvesting rice and cotton. Mary's mother wanted her to learn how to read and write. So when Mary was eleven years old, she walked eight miles each day to attend classes offered to African American children by the Presbyterian Church.

Mary was a gifted student. She was chosen by her

teacher to attend Scotia Seminary in North Carolina. Because she had good grades, she then received a scholarship to the Moody Bible Institute in Chicago, Illinois. Mary trained to be a missionary in Africa. But instead of traveling overseas, she decided to help the needy in her own country. She returned to Mayesville and began teaching.

Education Is the Key

Mary McLeod taught at many schools during the next several years. In 1898, she married Albertus Bethune; the following year, she gave birth to a son, Albert. In October 1904, Mary McLeod Bethune opened her own school, called the Daytona Normal and Industrial School for Negro Girls, in Daytona Beach, Florida.

At first, Bethune's school was held in her home and had only five students. She taught the girls how to read and write, as well as how to cook and sew. The school was very successful, so Bethune started expanding. Soon the school had more than 400 pupils—both girls and boys—and was moved to 14 buildings on a 23-acre campus. In 1923, Bethune's school merged with the

> "From the first, I made my learning, what little it was, useful every way I could."
>
> —Mary McLeod Bethune

Cookman Institute in Jacksonville, becoming Bethune-Cookman College.

During the 1920s, Bethune offered night classes to adults so that they could pass tests in order to vote in elections. This angered many white hate groups, whose members believed that blacks should not be allowed to vote. Bethune continued classes, even after being threatened and bullied. She became a champion of civil rights for African Americans across the U.S.

Influencing Presidents—and a Nation

Bethune fought for the rights of African Americans, becoming a leader and spokesperson for many groups,

---

TOPICAL TIDBIT

Women's Army Auxiliary Corps (WAAC)

In 1941, during World War II, Representative Edith Nourse Rogers of Massachusetts introduced a bill into Congress calling for a women's branch of the U.S. Army. On May 15, 1942, it became law and the Women's Army Auxiliary Corps—later known as the Women's Army Corps—was born. The many women who enlisted in the corps were known as WACs (pronounced *wax*). As adviser to the Secretary of War, Mary McLeod Bethune fought discrimination by ensuring that African American women were among those selected to become WAC officers.

including the National Association of Colored Women and the National Urban League. President Calvin Coolidge took notice of Bethune's work and appointed her to the Child Welfare Conference in 1928. In 1932, she was appointed to the White House Conference on Child Health by President Herbert Hoover. She then served as President Franklin D. Roosevelt's Special Adviser on Minority Affairs between 1936 and 1944. Roosevelt named her director of the National Youth Administration's Negro Affairs division, making Bethune the first African American woman to head a federal-level government agency.

Bethune used her influence with President Roosevelt to promote more blacks into leadership roles in the U.S. government. She formed a small group of leading African Americans that met often to discuss politics in Washington.

LIFE EVENTS

1875
Mary Jane McLeod is born near Mayesville South Carolina.

October 1904
Bethune opens a school in Daytona Beach, Florida.

1935-1949
Bethune founds and serves as president of the National Council of Negro Women (NCNW).

1936-1944
Bethune serves as Director of Negro Affairs under President Roosevelt.

1945
Bethune serves as a consultant on interracial understanding at a conference that leads to the establishment of the United Nations.

1955
Mary McLeod Bethune dies.

Bethune's group, which became the Federal Council on Negro Affairs, was often referred to as the "Black Cabinet." They met with top government officials to help create a better life for blacks in the U.S.

A Lifetime of Achievement

During her lifetime, Mary McLeod Bethune helped many people improve their lives through education. For this she received numerous awards and honors, including the Thomas Jefferson Award for leadership. In 1973, she was inducted into the National Women's Hall of Fame. After Bethune's death on May 18, 1955, her home in Washington, D.C., was turned into a national historic site.

Elizabeth Blackwell
First Female Doctor
(born 1821 • died 1910)

Elizabeth Blackwell was the first woman to earn a medical degree in the United States. Through her determination and hard work, she broke down barriers, inspiring and leading other women into the medical profession.

Becoming a Teacher

Elizabeth Blackwell was born on February 3, 1821, in Counterslip, England. When Elizabeth was 11 years old, her family moved to the United States. They lived for several years in the New York City area before moving to Cincinnati, Ohio. Elizabeth's father hired private tutors to teach his children.

In the late 1830s, Elizabeth and her sisters opened a private school. This was the beginning of long teaching careers for Elizabeth and her sister Emily. Elizabeth eventually left her family home to teach in Kentucky, North Carolina, and South Carolina. While she was in the Carolinas, Elizabeth Blackwell began learning about medicine from country doctors. She wanted to learn more.

Becoming a Doctor

In 1847, Blackwell applied to several medical schools, including Harvard and Yale, but was refused. At that time, women did not study medicine; it was considered a male profession. Blackwell believed that she could be a good doctor, even a surgeon, if given the chance. Finally, in 1848, she was accepted to Geneva Medical College (now Hobart and William Smith Colleges) in Geneva, New York.

Blackwell got into medical school on a fluke. The admission board thought that someone was pulling a prank by sending a woman's name to the medical school. Playing along, the board asked the students to vote whether or not they would like a woman among them. Not taking it very seriously, the students said yes. They were all surprised when Blackwell arrived.

Many of Blackwell's classmates did not want a woman to become a doctor and they were mean to her. Her teachers would not let her participate in classroom activities. Later, however, when they saw

> "If society will not admit of woman's free development, then society must be remodeled."
>
> —Elizabeth Blackwell

Elizabeth Blackwell

how seriously she took school, they supported her. Blackwell graduated from Geneva Medical College in 1849. She was the top-ranked student of the class.

Blackwell continued her studies in England and France. While in Paris, she got an eye infection, which left her blind in one eye. This dashed her hopes of becoming a surgeon.

In 1851, Blackwell returned to New York to practice medicine. No one would hire a female doctor, so she raised money and opened her own clinic in a poor section of New York City. At first, she had few patients. She wrote and lectured about the importance of cleanliness, and people began coming to her when they needed medical care. In 1857, together with her younger sister Emily—who had also become a doctor—and Dr. Marie Zakrzewska, Blackwell opened the New York Infirmary of Women and Children.

Teaching Medicine to Women

For the next several years, Elizabeth Blackwell traveled throughout Europe lecturing on "Medicine as a Profession for Ladies." The lectures were based on a series of papers that she wrote and published in 1852, called *The Laws of Life, With Special Reference to the Physical Education of Girls*.

During the Civil War (1861–1865), Blackwell founded the Women's Central Association of Relief, which

---

TOPICAL TIDBIT

A Place to Study

The Women's Medical College of the New York Infirmary was one of the first medical schools in the U.S. geared to teaching women. Opened in 1868 by Elizabeth and Emily Blackwell, with the help of Florence Nightingale, the college remained in operation for more than 30 years.

trained nurses to care for wounded soldiers. In 1868, the Blackwell sisters opened the Women's Medical College of the New York Infirmary. Shortly afterward, Elizabeth Blackwell returned to England, leaving Emily in charge.

Between 1875 and 1907, Elizabeth Blackwell taught classes in women's health at the London School of Medicine for Women. She died on May 31, 1910 in Sussex, England, and was buried in Scotland.

Blazing the Way

Blackwell spread her influence by writing a number of books on medicine, as well as an autobiography. As the first woman to receive a medical degree in the U.S., she opened the doors of medicine to women throughout the world. A statue honoring her stands on the campus of Hobart and William Smith Colleges.

LIFE EVENTS

1821
Elizabeth Blackwell is born in Counterslip, England.

1849
Blackwell graduates from Geneva Medical School in New York.

1853
Blackwell opens a private medical clinic in New York City.

1868
Elizabeth and Emily Blackwell open the Women's Medical College of the New York Infirmary.

1869
Blackwell moves back to England.

1895
Blackwell publishes her autobiography.

1910
Elizabeth Blackwell dies in Sussex, England.

Nellie Bly
(Elizabeth Cochrane Seaman)
Journalist
(born 1867? • died 1922)

Nellie Bly was a famous reporter who wrote about important social issues of her day—including the plight of the mentally ill, the poor, and working women. Casting light on the difficulties faced by her subjects, she wrote articles that brought about social reform (improvement) by government officials and private citizens. Bly worked to improve the role of women in society, daring to show that women could be independent and adventurous. Beginning in 1889, she traveled around the world in 72 days—alone.

Independent Spirit

Elizabeth Cochran was born in Cochran's Mills, Pennsylvania, on May 5—probably in 1867, though historians are not sure of the year. She was the daughter of Michael Cochran, a wealthy businessman, and his second wife. She was called Nellie by her family.

(She later added an *e* to Cochran because she thought it looked more sophisticated.) When Nellie was six, her father died, and the family fell on hard times.

As Nellie grew up, she wanted to pursue a career outside the home to help her mother. However, she lived in an era when "proper women" were supposed to be wives and mothers only, not career women. After she and her mother moved to the industrial city of Pittsburgh, Pennsylvania, Nellie learned a lot about the working classes, including female factory workers.

"Lonely Orphan Girl" Becomes Nellie Bly

In the mid-1880s, a *Pittsburgh Dispatch* columnist wrote a negative piece about women, called "What Girls Are Good For," stating that women were ill-suited for careers. Nellie sent an angry letter, signed "Lonely Orphan Girl," to the editor. The editor was impressed with her writing and hired her as a reporter.

Few women of the day used their real names when writing for publication, so the newspaper called her "Nellie Bly" after a famous song by Stephen Foster. Bly began writing about female factory workers and the poor. She even traveled to Mexico to report on poverty there. Bly's reporting on controversial topics angered powerful people, who put pressure on the newspaper. After that, she was assigned to "women's" subjects, such as fashion and cooking.

> "If we want good work from others or wish to accomplish anything ourselves, it will never do to harbor a doubt as to the result of an enterprise."
> —Nellie Bly

Unhappy with her situation in Pittsburgh, Nellie Bly headed to New York in search of a new job. An editor at the *New York World* gave her an assignment, daring her to go undercover at a home for mentally ill women. Bly had herself committed to the mental institution for 10 days, then wrote a detailed report of the conditions she experienced there, which included terrible health care, inedible food, unclean conditions, and cruel treatment. Her articles were later published as *Ten Days in a Mad House*. Bly's undercover reporting, among the first of its kind by any reporter, male or female, led to improvements at mental-health facilities.

Around the World in 72 Days

Bly continued to break new ground, reporting—from firsthand experience—on conditions in prison, a chorus line, and a sweatshop. Then she told her

---

TOPICAL TIDBIT

Father of Science Fiction

French author Jules Verne wrote the book *Around the World in 80 Days*. Many of his books tell futuristic tales with heroes using advanced technologies. Considered the father of science fiction, Verne wrote *Journey to the Center of the Earth* and *20,000 Leagues Under the Sea*, among others.

editors that she wanted to travel around the world, like the fictional hero Phileas Fogg in Jules Verne's popular novel, *Around the World in 80 Days*. The editors were against the idea, thinking that a man should make the trip. She finally convinced them to let her go, however, and Nellie Bly became the first person, male or female, to complete such a trek so quickly.

Bly's journey began on November 14, 1889. Her plan was to visit London, England; Singapore; Brindisi, Italy; and Hong Kong. She traveled by ship, train, carriage, and other means as she attempted to beat Fogg's fictional time of 80 days. In

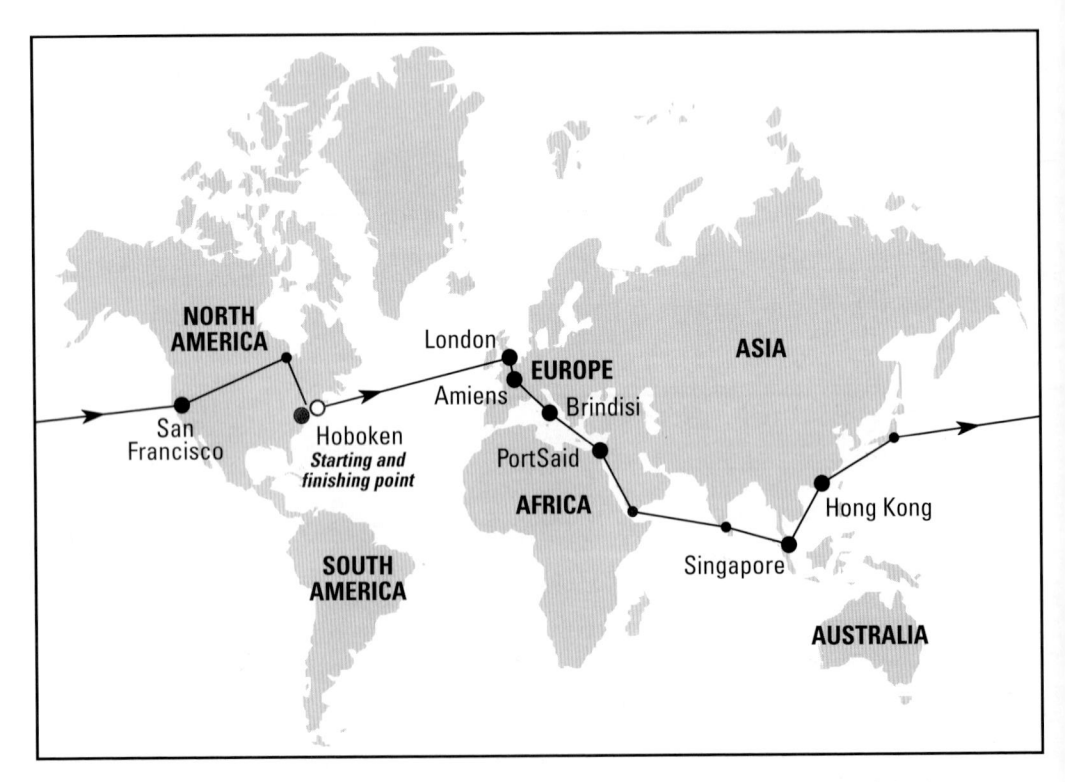

This map shows major stops on Bly's record-setting world trip.

the process, she met author Jules Verne himself. When she returned to New York, she was greeted by cheering fans. She had set a record: 72 days, 6 hours, 11 minutes, and 14 seconds. At age 25, she had become the most famous reporter in the country.

A Life Well Spent

In 1895, Bly retired from journalism and married millionaire Robert Seaman. He died 10 years later. Bly managed his business and created programs to help the workers improve their health and education. Later in life, she returned to reporting. She died on January 27, 1922.

Full of spirit and ambition, Nellie Bly broke many of the barriers that society put upon women in the late 19th century. She showed the world how courageous and determined a woman can be.

LIFE EVENTS

1867?
Elizabeth Cochran is born in Cochran's Mills, Pennsylvania.

1885
Nellie Bly is hired as a reporter for the *Pittsburgh Dispatch*.

1889-1890
Bly makes her famous trip around the world in 72 days for Pulitzer's newspaper, the *World*.

1895
Bly marries Robert Seaman, a millionaire businessman.

1904
After her husband's death, Bly takes control of his factory and insists on providing equal pay for female workers.

1922
Bly dies in New York, New York.

Margaret Bourke-White
Photojournalist
(born 1906 • died 1971)

It is often said that "one picture paints a thousand words." Such is the case of photographs taken by Margaret Bourke-White. A pioneer in the field of photojournalism, she traveled throughout the world, with camera in hand, telling stories about people and places through her photographs.

Architecture and Industry

Margaret White was born on June 14, 1906, in New York City. She grew up in the small New Jersey town of Bound Brook. Margaret's father was an inventor who designed printing presses. Margaret traveled with him to factories where he set up his machines. Later, when Margaret began her career as a professional photographer, her first subjects were industrial machines.

After graduating from Cornell University in 1927,

Margaret Bourke-White

Margaret began a career as a photographer. She wanted a professional sounding name—one that would be remembered easily. She chose to combine her mother's maiden name, Bourke, with her father's name, White.

In 1929, Henry Luce, the publisher of *Time* magazine, asked Margaret Bourke-White to join the staff of *Fortune*, his new magazine. She also worked with Luce as a photographer for *Life* magazine. The magazines featured photo-essays—groups of photographs that told a story without much text.

Bourke-White's first subjects were buildings and machinery, such as the Chrysler Building in New York, the Fort Peck dam in Montana, and the Krupp Iron Works in Germany. Pictures of industrial sites in the Soviet Union were the basis for her 1934 book, *U.S.S.R.: A Portfolio of*

Photographs. She also produced documentary films on the Soviet Union, entitled *Eyes on Russia* and *Red Republic*.

In 1935, Bourke-White met the author Erskine Caldwell, who was famous for his novels *Tobacco Road* and *God's Little Acre*. Bourke-White and Caldwell worked together on several projects—he wrote the text and she took the photographs. The most famous work they did together is called *You Have Seen Their Faces*. The book, published in 1937, shows what life was like in the Deep South during the Great Depression. Bourke-White and Caldwell were married in 1939, but divorced a few years later.

> "The beauty of the past belongs in the past."
> —Margaret Bourke-White, on modern photography

Bourke-White Goes to War

When World War II (1939-1945) broke out in Europe, Bourke-White wanted to be one of the first photographers on the scene. She boarded a ship for North Africa. The ship was struck by enemy torpedoes and sank, but Bourke-White survived unharmed and finished the trip. Through her photographs in *Life* magazine, she showed the American public events faced daily by the average soldier.

Bourke-White continued photographing the horrors of war as a correspondent. Working with U.S. military forces, she was chosen to travel with the troops of U.S. General George S. Patton into the Buchenwald death camp, which had been operated by the Nazis.

Inside the camp, Bourke-White was sickened by what she saw. She wrote, "I saw and photographed the piles of naked, lifeless bodies, the human skeletons in furnaces, the living skeletons who would die the next day because they had had to wait too long for deliverance." Her photographs were used to bring to justice the men who had committed crimes of war.

Later in Life

After the war's end, Bourke-White was given many new assignments for *Life*, including a two-year mission to interview and photograph Mohandas K. Gandhi, a

---

TOPICAL TIDBIT

Life Magazine

Henry Luce, the owner of Time-Life Books, published several magazines, including *Time* and *Life*. After 36 years of publication, *Life* was laid to rest in 1972, due to high printing costs. Time-Life Books continued to issue special editions. In the 1990s, *Life* magazine was returned to monthly publication. That ended in 2000. It is still published occasionally, to document special events.

leader of India's independence movement. During the Korean War (1950-1952), she served as a correspondent for the United Nations (UN).

In 1952, Bourke-White was diagnosed with Parkinson's disease, an illness that results in uncontrolled shaking. Her hands were no longer steady, so she could not hold a camera. She turned her talents to writing articles and books, taking photographs when she could. Bourke-White died on August 27, 1971, in Stamford, Connecticut.

The story of Margaret Bourke-White can be found in her autobiography, *Portrait of Myself*. Bourke-White's courage as one of the world's first photojournalists opened the door for others, especially women. Bourke-White's photographs are displayed in museums throughout the world.

LIFE EVENTS

1906
Margaret White is born in New York City.

1927
White begins her career with industrial photography in Ohio.

1929
Bourke-White begins work as a photographer for *Fortune* magazine.

1936-1969
Bourke-White works as a photographer for *Life* magazine.

1963
Bourke-White publishes her autobiography, *Portrait of Myself*.

1971
Margaret Bourke-White dies in Stamford, Connecticut.

Rachel Carson
Biologist and Environmentalist
(born 1907 • died 1964)

Rachel Carson grew up loving the natural world. As a biologist, she was one of the first people concerned about pollution and pesticides and their impact on Earth, animals, and humans. Her famous book, *Silent Spring*, warned people about the dangers of chemicals. Today she is considered the mother of modern environmentalism.

> "Those who dwell, as scientists or laymen, among the beauties and mysteries of the earth are never alone or weary of life."
> —Rachel Carson

Science or Writing?

Born May 27, 1907, in Springdale, Pennsylvania, Rachel Louise Carson loved to explore her family's land. Her mother encouraged her love of nature.

Rachel also had a natural talent for writing, and at 10 years old, she began sending her stories to children's magazines.

The Carsons had little money, but they had enough to send Rachel to the Pennsylvania College for

Women (now Chatham College). Rachel studied writing and literature, but was also required to take science courses. She loved science, and changed her major from writing to zoology (the study of animals). Her decision caused concern on campus, because many people at that time considered science to be a man's field. Rachel graduated in 1929.

Rachel Carson continued her studies at Johns Hopkins University, receiving a master's degree in zoology in 1932. Three years later, her father died, so Carson needed to earn enough money to support her mother. She found work at the U.S. Bureau of Fisheries (later the U.S. Fish and Wildlife Service) writing radio scripts. Her job combined her main interests—science and writing.

Writing About the Sea

In all, Carson worked for the Fisheries Bureau for about 15 years. During that time, her sister died and Carson began to raise her sister's two children. Carson never married.

She began researching oceans for her radio program. This research led to the publication of articles and several books, including *Under the Sea-Wind*, *The Sea Around Us*, and *The Edge of the Sea*. Carson's writing was popular with readers because she told the scientific story of nature in a way that most people could understand.

During World War II (1939-1945), shortages of food—particularly of beef and pork—were common. American women were looking for alternatives, and Carson provided just that. She prepared booklets that taught homemakers how to cook various fish dishes. By the early 1950s, Carson's books were bringing in enough money so that she could leave the Bureau and write full time. She and her mother settled in Maine, near the sea.

Warning of a "Silent Spring"

In 1958, Carson learned that birds were dying on a friend's property in Massachusetts. Carson thought it was caused by a chemical spray used to kill insects. Such sprays were used throughout the country to keep insects from destroying crops. Carson had heard about problems with chemical sprays while

TOPICAL TIDBIT

Chemical Sprays

Rachel Carson warned about the dangers of using chemical sprays, called pesticides. Pesticide sprays make it possible for farmers to send more crops to the market. They also help stop the spread of certain diseases. However, some sprays harm birds and animals. Some such chemicals eventually poison humans, too.

working with the Fisheries Bureau years earlier, so she decided to investigate further.

Carson discovered that while the chemicals did kill pesky insects, they also polluted the water and seeped into the food chain. Instead of killing only insects, the chemicals killed birds and other animals as well. Carson studied hundreds of reports and talked with many scientists about the chemicals. Then, in 1962, she compiled her research in a book called *Silent Spring*. It told of a day when no birds would be left to sing because they would have been killed off by chemicals.

Although Carson's facts were accurate, she received a lot of criticism, especially from chemical companies. They threatened her with lawsuits. Some people called her an "alarmist" and an "hysterical woman." But Carson had many supporters, too, including nature groups, such as the Audubon Society. President John F. Kennedy was another supporter. Influenced by *Silent Spring*, he appointed a special committee to study the uses and effects of pesticides. The debates between Carson's opponents and supporters caused more people to read her book and voice their concerns.

Her Work Made a Difference

Rachel Carson died of cancer on April 14, 1964, in Silver Spring, Maryland. She never knew the great impact that her book would have on the world. Because she had the courage to speak out, *ecology* and *environment* have become household words.

Rachel Carson is credited with inspiring the formation of the Environmental Protection Agency (EPA) and the creation of Earth Day. She was inducted into the National Women's Hall of Fame, and *Time* magazine named her one of the 100 most influential people of the 20th century.

LIFE EVENTS

1907
Rachel Louise Carson is born in Springdale, Pennsylvania.

1936-1951
Carson works for the U.S. Fish and Wildlife Service.

1941
Carson publishes *Under the Sea-Wind*.

1951
Carson publishes *The Sea Around Us*.

1962
Silent Spring, which details the potential problems of pesticides, is published.

1963
Carson testifies before Congress, calling for new measures to be taken to protect the natural environment.

1964
Carson dies of cancer.

Amelia Earhart
Pioneering Pilot
(born 1897 • died 1937?)

As one of the world's first female airplane pilots, Amelia Earhart showed that women were just as capable as men of flying airplanes. She became famous in an era when aviation was still new. At that time, most people had never flown in planes, nor did they think about traveling to foreign countries by air. Not only did Earhart fly planes, but she made several long distance flights across continents and oceans, with companions and alone.

Becoming a Pilot

Amelia Mary Earhart was born on July 24, 1897, in Atchison, Kansas. She saw her first airplane when she was 10 years old. It did not make much of an impression on her then, even though there were few aircraft in those days.

Amelia's parents separated in 1914, and Amelia and her sister, Muriel, went to live in Chicago with their mother. Around 1917, during World War I, Amelia headed to Canada to serve as a nurse at a Red Cross hospital.

> "As soon as we left the ground, I knew I myself had to fly!"
> —Amelia Earhart
> (on her first time in a plane)

Amelia left Canada to begin medical classes at Columbia University in New York City. However, she moved to California in 1920 to be with her parents, who had reunited. While there, she went to an air show with her father and went up in a plane. She loved it immediately and began to take lessons with Anita "Neta" Snook. After a few months, Amelia Earhart bought her first plane.

Flying Solo

Earhart competed in various air shows and set speed and altitude records. Because there were few air shows then, Earhart needed to find another job. She traveled to Boston in 1925 to work as a social worker. A year later, she was asked if she wanted to fly across the Atlantic Ocean—becoming the first woman to do so. She was eager to make the trip, which occurred on June 18, 1928. Earhart was only a passenger on this trip; the plane was piloted by Wilmer Stultz and Louis Gordon. However, when the flight was successful, Earhart became a celebrity, and she published her account of the trip in the book *20 Hours, 40 Minutes*.

During this time, Earhart met and married publisher George Putnam. She still wanted to fly into the record books herself. On May 20-21, 1932, Earhart flew across the Atlantic Ocean alone. She was the first woman to make the flight and had the fastest time.

Between her historic flights, Earhart took a job at Transcontinental Air Transport. It was her job to show

TOPICAL TIDBIT

Earning Her Wings

Amelia Earhart was not the only pilot making records in the early days of aviation. Jacqueline Cochran was another woman who broke records and worked as a test pilot. Cochran, who believed that women should help out in World War II (1939-1945), established the Women Air Force Service Pilots (WASPs).

other women that it was fun and comfortable to travel by plane. In January 1935, Earhart made another "first" flight—she flew across the Pacific Ocean from Hawaii to California. She was not only the first *woman* to make the flight successfully, but she was the first *person* to do so. All previous attempts had ended in disaster.

Mysterious Disappearance

In 1937, Earhart attempted to fly around the world. She took Fred Noonan along as her navigator.

Earhart waves good-bye as she leaves for her around-the-world flight.

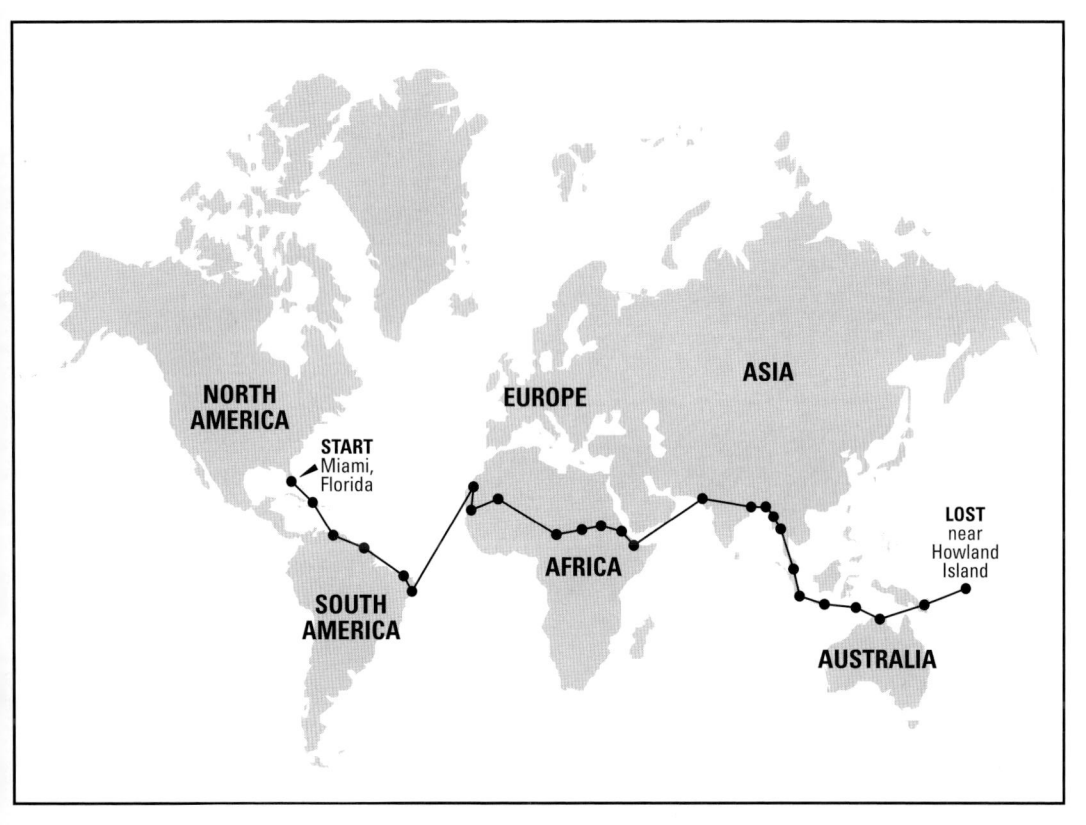

Earhart's flight plan included these stops.

Along the way, she wrote articles about her experiences and sent them off when they stopped to refuel. The articles were later published as *Last Flight*.

By July 2, Earhart and Noonan had completed 22,000 miles out of 29,000. They were heading to Howland Island in the Pacific Ocean on the last, most difficult leg of the trip. A U.S. Coast Guard cutter was near the island keeping track of Earhart and Noonan through radio contact. Earhart sent several messages, but did not seem able to hear the Coast

Guard's response. The plane never reached the island.

When the plane did not arrive, a massive search began. Earhart and Noonan had vanished without a trace.

No one knows what really happened. Some people say that Earhart was captured by the Japanese, who were getting ready to fight World War II. Others say that she landed on an island and lived with a fisherman for the rest of her life. Most believe that her plane crashed into the sea. Her death is listed as July 2, 1937, the day she and Noonan disappeared.

Earhart's Legacy

Amelia Earhart inspired other women to be adventurous and try flying. She made historic flights in a time when aviation was new. She was often the first person—male or female—to do so.

LIFE EVENTS

1897
Amelia Mary Earhart is born in Atchison, Kansas.

1920
Earhart takes her first airplane ride.

1932
Earhart becomes the first woman to fly solo across the Atlantic, and she sets a time record while doing so.

1935
Earhart becomes the first pilot ever to survive a cross-Pacific flight from Hawaii to California.

1937
Earhart departs on a round-the-world-flight.

1937
Earhart and her navigator disappear over the Pacific Ocean and are presumed dead.

Dian Fossey
Zoologist
(born 1932 • died 1985)

Most of what is known today about mountain gorillas comes from research conducted by Dian *(DEE-ahn)* Fossey. For more than 18 years, she lived with mountain gorillas in East Africa. She befriended them and ate with them. They became part of her family and they accepted Fossey as one of their own.

> "Immediately I was struck by the physical magnificence of the huge, jet-black bodies blended against the green."
>
> —Dian Fossey, on seeing mountain gorillas for the first time

Going to Africa

Dian Fossey was born on January 16, 1932, in San Francisco, California. She loved animals all her life. While in college, she studied veterinary science and occupational therapy. (Occupational therapy helps disabled people do everyday tasks.)

50 American Women

Dian Fossey holds a photo of one of the gorillas she studied, September 24, 1970.

Fossey had always longed to visit Africa. In 1963, she made the trip. While in eastern Africa, she met anthropologists Louis and Mary Leakey, who were searching for early human fossils. They discussed with Fossey how important it was to study apes in order to learn more about the evolution of humans.

Dian Fossey

Dian took particular interest in one type of ape, the endangered mountain gorilla.

When Fossey got back to the U.S., all she could think about was returning to Africa. In 1967, with the help of the Leakeys, she established the Karisoke Research Centre in Rwanda's Virunga Mountains. There, she studied gorillas in their natural environment.

Gorillas in the Mist

The Virunga Mountains border three African nations—Rwanda, Uganda, and Congo (formerly Zaire). Along the slopes of these mountains is a dense rain forest. The area is usually topped with a cold mist. Everything that Fossey needed for her research laboratory had to be carried up the mountain. She employed local men to help haul the equipment and

---

TOPICAL TIDBIT

Mountain Gorillas

Mountain gorillas are an endangered species, with only about 5,000 to 15,000 left in existence. They live in the rain forests of eastern, central Africa. The average male gorilla stands between five and six feet tall and weighs between 300 and 600 pounds. Females are much smaller. Gorillas walk on all four limbs, often leaning on their fists.

to work as cooks, guards, and trackers (to follow the tracks made by the gorillas).

At first, Fossey watched the gorillas from a distance. When they saw her, they were frightened. They would scream to warn the other gorillas, then run away. To get a closer look, Fossey used binoculars and spied on them from behind trees. Soon the gorillas got used to her presence and stopped running away. They ignored her as they ate thistles, celery, and blackberry leaves growing in the forest.

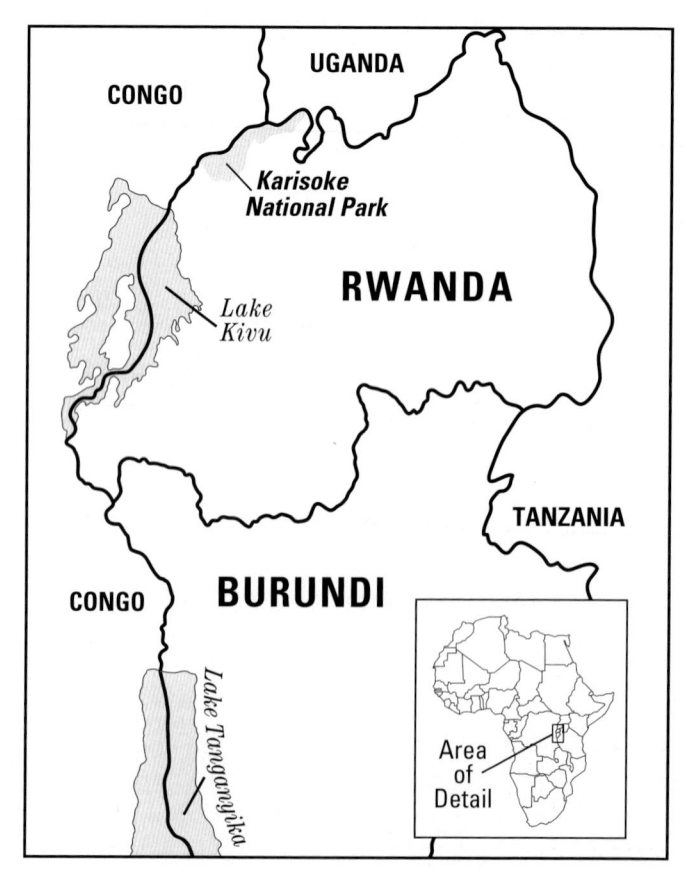

The Karisoke Research Center is in northwestern Rwanda.

Fossey watched the gorillas very closely, recording their habits in a notebook that she kept with her at all times. She could identify each gorilla by its markings and coloring, as well as its personal habits. She gave the gorillas names, such as Uncle Bert, Peanuts, and Digit. Uncle Bert was an older gorilla, with a lot of silver fur. Peanuts was a show-off, always beating his chest. He was the first gorilla to make personal contact with Fossey by touching her hand. Digit, however, was her favorite. He was very playful as a youngster and loved it when she tickled him. For nearly 18 years, Fossey watched Digit grow into an adult.

The Fight Against Poaching

On several occasions, Fossey returned to the U.S. She gave lectures about her work and was featured in *National Geographic* magazine. In the late 1970s, she became very outspoken about a terrible problem facing the mountain gorillas—poaching, which is the illegal killing of wild or endangered animals. Poachers were killing gorillas and cutting off the hands and feet to sell as ashtrays. Fossey became even more involved when her beloved Digit was killed by a poacher.

Fossey worked with Rwandan government officials to stop the poaching. She devoted much of her time and resources to patrolling the area surrounding the Karisoke Research Center to keep it free from poachers. On several occasions, Fossey caught poachers and scared them by pretending that she was a witch. The poachers hated her. On December 26, 1985, Fossey was found murdered in her cabin. Although her murderers were never found, many people believe that she was killed by poachers.

An Important Legacy

Dian Fossey's story was told in the 1988 film *Gorillas in the Mist*, based on her book of the same name.

She wrote in her diary, "I had a deep wish to see and live with wild animals in a world that hadn't yet been completely changed by humans." She got her wish, and in the process, advanced the understanding of one of man's closest living relatives. Fossey is buried in Rwanda, alongside Digit.

LIFE EVENTS

1932
Dian Fossey is born in San Francisco, California.

1963
Fossey takes a seven-week safari, her first trip to Africa.

1967
Fossey establishes the Karisoke Research Center in Rwanda.

1970-1974
Fossey completes her doctorate in zoology at Cambridge University in England.

1983
Fossey publishes her research for a general audience in *Gorillas in the Mist*.

1985
Dian Fossey is found dead in her hut in Rwanda.

Betty Friedan
Founder of the Feminist Movement
(born 1921 • died 2006)

Betty Friedan influenced the way women are treated in the United States. Her best-selling 1963 book, *The Feminine Mystique*, has been translated into many languages. Friedan's work with the National Organization for Women (NOW) inspired other women's-rights groups to fight for an end to the second-class status that women receive throughout the world.

> "A girl should not expect special privileges because of her sex, but neither should she adjust to prejudice and discrimination."
> —Betty Friedan

Becoming a Feminist

Betty Naomi Goldstein was born in Peoria, Illinois, on February 4, 1921. She graduated from Smith College in 1942, with a degree in psychology.

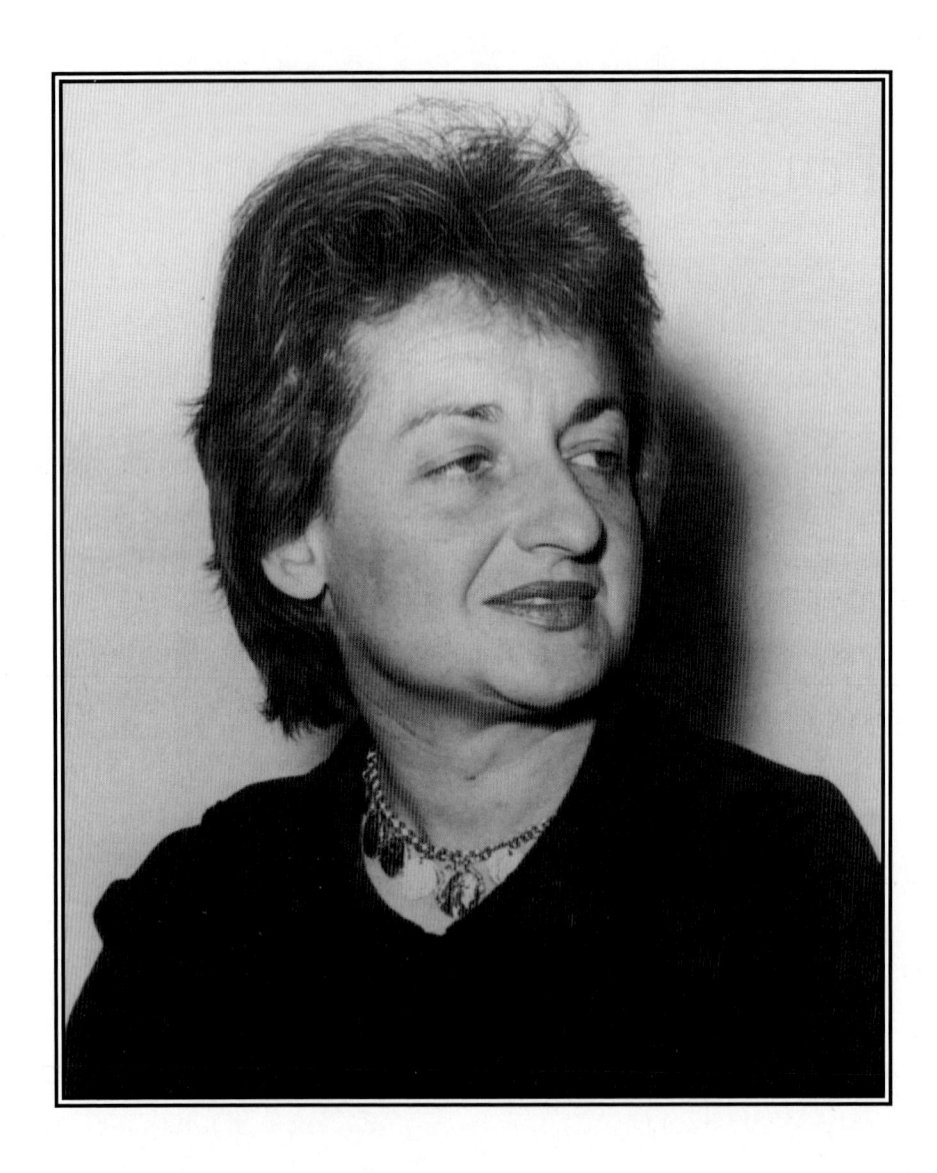

Betty moved to New York City, where she met, and later married, Carl Friedan. The couple had three children, and Betty became a devoted wife and mother.

During the 1950s, however, Betty Friedan was not satisfied with being a homemaker. She wanted to do more, but had always been taught that she should be content to be a wife and mother. Women were told that they should be happy at home. Women should not seek personal satisfaction through their own accomplishments, but be happy with the accomplishments of their husbands and children.

In 1957, Friedan used her knowledge of psychology to create a questionnaire that asked women if they were personally fulfilled with being homemakers. She asked her classmates from Smith College to complete the questionnaire. The results of the survey were revealing—Friedan was not alone. Many other women were unhappy with their limited role in society.

The Feminine Mystique

In 1963, Friedan compiled the results of her surveys and wrote *The Feminine Mystique*. In the book, she discussed "the problem that has no name"—the dissatisfaction of women who were forced to live out their dreams through their husbands and children, rather than through accomplishments of their own. According to Friedan, women were strongly discouraged from pursuing other choices, such as careers, because their role in society was that of wife and mother.

Friedan also noted that women were discriminated against by men and by society as a whole. For instance, women were paid lower salaries than men were, even if they did the same work. If a woman chose to focus on her career instead of getting married and having children, she was considered too independent. If a woman was married with children and chose to work, she was thought by many to be a bad mother. Society, in general, did not believe that a woman could do both.

Friedan thought that women deserved better, and that women needed to break these unfair stereotypes. *The Feminine Mystique* was an overnight success, causing many women to reevaluate their lives.

Making Policy, Not Coffee

In 1966, Friedan founded the National Organization for Women (NOW). The group's mission was to gain rights for women that were equal to those given to men, especially in the workplace. Under Friedan's leadership, the group worked to

TOPICAL TIDBIT

Women's Rights Throughout the World

In the United States and Europe, women's-rights issues mostly relate to employment practices. In other parts of the world, however, a woman must fight for more basic rights, such as the right to prosecute a man who beats her, the right to get an education, and the right to hold a job.

remove qualifications on job applications that were based on gender. Still strong, NOW continues the struggle to get women elected to government office, to create day-care facilities for working mothers, to set up family-planning centers, to gain pregnancy leave from employers, and to get pensions for women. In 2005, the group boasted more than 500,000 members, both women and men.

Friedan also played an active role in the formation of the National Women's Political Caucus in 1971. She believed that women should be more active in the political arena— "to make policy, not coffee." One of the major achievements of the Caucus was to call for the Equal Rights Amendment (ERA) to the U.S. Constitution, which demanded equal pay for equal work. Despite a tough fight, the ERA failed to pass in 1982.

LIFE EVENTS

1921
Betty Naomi Goldstein is born in Peoria, Illinois.

1963
Friedan publishes *The Feminine Mystique*.

1966
Friedan founds the National Organization for Women (NOW).

1996
Friedan publishes *The Fountain of Age*, which calls for fair treatment of the elderly.

1998 - 2001
Friedan directs *The New Paradigm Project: Women, Men, Work, Family, and Public Policy*.

2006
Friedan dies of congestive heart failure.

However, since that time, 35 states have ratified it as part of their state constitution.

New Politics

Some 30 years after *The Feminine Mystique* was published, Friedan was still going strong. She wrote several more books, including *Beyond Gender: The New Politics of Work and Family*, published in 1997. In *The New Politics*, Friedan wrote that men and women must put aside gender issues and work together to overcome the negative impact of economics on the quality of family life. The ideas expressed in her book made Friedan the perfect choice as a guest lecturer at Cornell University's Institute for Women and Work.

Betty Friedan died of heart failure on February 4, 2006—her 85th birthday. By establishing NOW and the National Women's Political Caucus, and through her books and lectures, Friedan influenced the treatment of women around the world. She remains a role model for women and girls everywhere.

Althea Gibson
Tennis Champion
(born 1927 • died 2003)

Until the mid-20th century, African-American athletes were not allowed to participate in many amateur and professional sporting competitions in the United States. The major teams and tournaments in the country were open only to white players. However, in the late 1940s and early 1950s, black players, such as baseball's Jackie Robinson and tennis's Althea Gibson, crossed the color line. Finally, athletes of color were allowed to compete with other top players from around the world. On the tennis court, Althea Gibson proved that she was an exceptional athlete.

A Welcomed Escape

Althea Gibson was born on August 25, 1927, in Silver, South Carolina. Her family, which was poor, moved to New York City in 1930. In New York, Althea had trouble in school. She did not like going to classes and often skipped school. She always got in trouble for it when she got home.

◇ 50 American Women ◇

Sports provided Althea with an escape from her troubles. She enjoyed table tennis (Ping-Pong), and got some instruction through public programs at local parks. Then a friend gave her a tennis racket. Althea discovered a natural talent and love for tennis.

Althea Gibson

In those days, however, tennis was considered a sport for wealthy white people. There were separate clubs, sports facilities, and matches for black players and white players. No matter how good an African American athlete played the game, he or she was not allowed to compete with whites.

Althea did not care about the race issues. She loved the game. In 1941, she began taking lessons at the Harlem Cosmopolitan Tennis Club, an organization for African American players.

> "No matter what accomplishments you make, someone helped you."
> —Althea Gibson

Rising Star

Althea Gibson quickly showed her skill in tennis. In 1942, she won the all-black American Tennis Association (ATA) tournament. Eventually Gibson dropped out of school. In 1946, however, Dr. Hubert Eaton became interested in 19-year-old Gibson's tennis career. He took her to North Carolina to live, study, and take tennis lessons. A year later, Gibson again became the ATA National Champion—a title that she held for 10 years. Still, she was denied the right to compete in major international competitions.

In the late 1940s, doors began to open for African Americans. In 1947, Jackie Robinson became the first black player to join a major-league baseball team. Gibson was not far behind. A white tennis player named Alice Marble complained to readers of *American Lawn Tennis* magazine that discrimination was keeping talented athletes like Gibson from competing against the finest players in the world. The tennis community took notice, and Gibson was invited to enter the tennis competition at Forest Hills in New York in 1950. She became the first African American to compete in that contest.

From that point on, Gibson was given more invitations to compete, and she took advantage of the offers. In 1951, she became the first African American to compete at Wimbledon, in England. In 1956, she became the first black player to win the French Open. That same year, she participated in a

TOPICAL TIDBIT

The Williams Sisters

Althea Gibson paved the way for two of tennis's current superstars: Venus and Serena Williams. Each sister plays singles tennis and mixed doubles; together, they make up one of the most formidable doubles teams around. In 2000, they posted a 15-0 record for doubles and became the first sister team to win an Olympic gold medal for doubles tennis.

goodwill tour of Southeast Asia, sponsored by the U.S. State Department. In 1957, she rose to the top of her profession by winning major championships at Wimbledon and the U.S. Open. When she returned to New York, a ticker-tape parade was held in her honor.

Other Pursuits

In 1953, Gibson graduated from Florida A&M University. In 1957, she showcased her singing talents at a dinner during that year's Wimbledon tournament. Two years later, she recorded an album called *Althea Gibson Sings*.

Gibson was a well-rounded athlete. Soon after she retired from tennis competition, in 1958, she took up golf. She was so good that she joined the Ladies Professional Golf Association (LPGA) in 1964, and competed

LIFE EVENTS

1927
Althea Gibson is born in Silver, South Carolina.

1942-1952
Gibson is the American Tennis Association's National Champion.

1950
Gibson is invited to compete at a competition with white players in Forest Hills, New York.

1951
Gibson is the first African American to compete at Wimbledon.

1957
Gibson wins at Wimbledon and the U.S. Open.

1964
Gibson joins the Ladies Professional Golf Association (LPGA).

2003
Gibson dies.

in golf tournaments. Gibson married Will Darben in 1965. Ten years later, she took a job with the New Jersey Department of Recreation.

Inducted into many sports halls of fame, Gibson also worked with the Althea Gibson Foundation, an organization that helps city children learn more about golf and tennis. After ailing for some time, Gibson died on September 28, 2003. Althea Gibson will be long remembered for breaking the color barrier in tennis, clearing the path for other African American athletes.

Katharine Graham
Publisher
(born 1917 • died 2001)

During a time when many American women didn't work outside the home, Katharine Graham became head of the *Washington Post* newspaper. Under Graham's leadership, the *Post* broke several major political stories. Pressured by government officials, her lawyers, and the paper's accountants to not publish the articles, Graham stood steadfast and let the stories be printed. She believed that people deserved to know the truth. Through her courage and moral conviction, Graham led the *Post* to become one of the leading newspapers in the world.

A Life of Privilege

Katharine Meyer was born on June 16, 1917, in New York City. She was the daughter of wealthy and successful parents,

> "I became absorbed by the challenge, I was trying to learn all the time, and I loved what I was doing."
> —Katharine Graham

who were frequently away. As a child, Katharine was shy and sometimes lacked self-esteem. In 1933, her father, Eugene Meyer, purchased the *Washington Post* newspaper, which was having financial trouble. Katharine studied at Vassar College and graduated from the University of Chicago in 1938 before getting a job as a reporter in San Francisco. Before she married law clerk Philip Graham in 1940, she worked for awhile at the *Post*, her father's newspaper.

But once she started having children—four in all—she left working life to focus on raising her children and taking care of her husband. At the time, society discouraged women, especially mothers, from working outside the home. When Eugene Meyer retired from the *Post* in 1946, he needed someone to replace him. Despite Katharine's interest and experience in journalism, he chose her husband, Philip, to take the helm. Meyer told his daughter that men were not supposed to work for their wives.

Although he was smart and popular, Philip Graham struggled with mental illness. In 1963, Katharine became a widow when her husband took his own life. This left the *Post*, which had become a successful newspaper, in Katharine's hands.

Rising to the Challenge

Managing a major daily newspaper is a huge task. In some ways, the job was intimidating to Katharine Graham. At first, she felt insecure, especially being the only woman in a major leadership role at the paper. But she stepped up to the challenge. She decided to learn as much as she could about the operation. She eventually hired Ben Bradlee as managing

> "I had very little idea of what I was supposed to be doing, so I set out to learn. What I essentially did was to put one foot in front of the other, shut my eyes, and step off the edge."
> —Katharine Graham

editor. Under Graham and Bradlee, the *Post* began to delve deeply into investigative stories.

In 1971, the *Post* ran one of the most important political stories of the era. A worker at the Pentagon had turned over secret government documents about the United States's involvement in the controversial Vietnam War. Although the government tried to keep "The Pentagon Papers" from being published, Graham went with the story. By doing what she believed was right, Graham made the paper more successful, but also made some enemies in government.

A year later, the *Post* became involved in a story so big that it changed the leadership of the United States.

TOPICAL TIDBIT

Amelia Jenks Bloomer and the *Lily*

Amelia Jenks Bloomer (1818-1894) published the *Lily*, a women's newspaper in New York. The publication ran articles on temperance (against alcohol) and women's rights. Bloomer is remembered for her style of dress. At that time, women wore bulky, floor-length dresses. But Bloomer encouraged women to wear pantalettes (puffy pants) because they were more comfortable. She told her female employees to wear pants because long skirts could get caught in printing machines. Such pants came to be called "bloomers."

Bringing Down the President

In 1972, *Post* reporters Bob Woodward and Carl Bernstein investigated a break-in at the Democratic National Committee headquarters, located in the Watergate Hotel in Washington, D.C. As the journalists looked deeper and deeper into the crime, the clues led them to presidential aides at the White House. Graham knew that the "Watergate" story would have a major impact, so she made sure that her reporters were fair and accurate. She stood by her reporters and the work they had done.

Many people, including government officials and Graham's lawyers, advised her to abandon the story. They said that it would bring the *Post* financial ruin. But, Graham trusted her instincts and ran it anyway. The *Post* was the first paper to report the story. After the Watergate scandal became front-page news, President Richard M. Nixon eventually resigned from office. The *Post* won many major awards, including the Pulitzer Prize. Although the reporters received much praise for their work, Bernstein said that Graham was the true hero.

Graham led the *Post* until 1979 when she turned over the role of publisher to her son Donald. She continued to serve the Washington Post Company as chairman of the board and chief executive officer. During her years at the *Post*, she hired more women and minorities, giving others the chance to excel. In 1997, her autobiography, *Personal History*, was published. She won the Pulitzer Prize for her best-selling book.

In July of 2001, Graham visited Idaho to attend a conference. She took a bad fall and died several days later on July 17. She was 84. People remember Graham for the fairness, courage, and moral conviction she showed when exposing government corruption. But, her contribution is all the more important because she made it at a time when women were still being discouraged from getting involved in business and politics.

LIFE EVENTS

1917
Katharine Meyer is born in New York City.

1946
Katharine's husband, Philip Graham, becomes publisher of the *Washington Post*.

1963
Katharine takes over the *Post*.

1971
The *Post* publishes "The Pentagon Papers."

1972
The *Post* exposes the Watergate scandal.

1997
Graham publishes *Personal History*, an autobiography, for which she wins the Pulitzer Prize.

2001
Graham dies in Sun Valley, Idaho.

Martha Graham
Founder of Modern Dance
(born 1894 • died 1991)

Martha Graham took the American dance scene by storm, developing a new style and technique that was bold and innovative. Graham's stark choreography brought out the innermost emotions of the characters dancing on the stage and was a major influence on American dance of the 20th century. Some even call her the mother of modern American dance.

Martha Wants to Dance

Martha Graham was born in Allegheny (now Pittsburgh), Pennsylvania, on May 11, 1894. When she was a young girl, she wanted to dance. Her father forbid her to go to dance school, but dancing was in her blood.

When she turned 22, Graham enrolled in the Denishawn School of Dancing in Los Angeles, California. The school taught modern dance, using a combination of ballet movements and folk dancing from countries around the world. The Denishawn

50 American Women

Martha Graham rehearses with her partner and husband,
Erick Hawkins, in New York City, 1950.

dance company wore exotic costumes to create a feeling of other-worldliness for the audience.

Graham toured with the Denishawn troupe for seven years. In 1923, she moved to New York City—the hub of dance in America. Then she took a teaching post at the Eastman School of Music in Rochester, New York, and, after two years, was named director of the dance department. All the while, Graham kept dancing. She appeared in the Greenwich Village Follies from 1923 to 1925.

Her Own Dance Company

While living in New York, Graham decided that it was time to start her own dance company. To raise money, Graham modeled clothing, danced at the opening of the Radio City Music Hall in New York, and taught actors—including Gregory Peck and Bette Davis—how to move on the big screen.

> "Dance is the hidden language of the soul for the body."
> —Martha Graham

Graham started her own dance company for women in 1929. Graham's technique was new. Her dances included stark, angular movements, that showed the emotions of the characters. It was harsh and dramatic, and different from anything anyone had seen before. Critics did not like it, but audiences loved it.

Although Graham loved to dance, she eventually turned to choreography (composing dances). Graham used costumes, music, stage designs, and lighting to set the scene for the dance. She taught the women in her troupe dance steps, arm movements, and facial expressions that brought their characters to life.

Most of the time, Graham wrote the story line for the

dance herself. Many of the dances highlighted famous women throughout history, including Joan of Arc, Emily Dickinson, Charlotte and Emily Brontë, and women from Greek mythology.

To add to the overall experience for the audience, Graham hired famous composers Louis Horst and Aaron Copland to write the music for several of her productions. She also commissioned Isamu Noguchi, a well-known sculptor and designer, to create sets for the stage—something that had never been done before.

No Stopping Martha

Graham never stopped dancing. In all, she choreographed nearly 150 dance productions, appearing as the lead dancer in most of them. She gave her final

---

TOPICAL TIDBIT

Aaron Copland

Composer Aaron Copland worked with Martha Graham on the Broadway musical *Appalachian Spring* in 1944. Copland composed many musical scores that reflect the American frontier. He is most noted for *Fanfare for the Common Man* and for *Rodeo*, which includes the foot-tapping "Hoedown"—a compilation of American folk ballads.

stage performance in 1968 at the age of 74.

When she was 90 years old, Graham choreographed a dance to the musical piece *Rite of Spring*. *Rite of Spring*, composed in 1913 by the Russian-American composer Igor Stravinsky, is one of the first pieces of modern music. In 1984, the National Endowment for the Arts funded an effort to put Graham's teachings on film.

Dancing Queen

Martha Graham died on April 1, 1991. Her unique choreography changed the course of American dance. Through sharp movements, creative stage designs, and modern music, she transformed traditional dance productions into emotional representations of the stories being told. Her efforts were rewarded in 1976, when she received the Presidential Medal of Freedom, the highest honor given in the U.S.

LIFE EVENTS

1894
Martha Graham is born in Allegheny (now Pittsburgh), Pennsylvania.

1916
Graham enters the Denishawn School of Dancing.

1923
Graham moves to New York and later begins teaching.

1929
Graham begins her own dance company.

1944
Graham choreographs and performs in *Appalachian Spring*.

1991
Martha Graham dies.

Ella Grasso
First Female Governor in the United States
(born 1919 • died 1981)

Ella Grasso devoted her life to the people of Connecticut. She believed in working-class people and they believed in her. They elected her the first female governor of that state. As Grasso advanced up the political ladder, she never lost an election. She served the people of Connecticut for 28 years and is an inspiration to all women in politics.

> "It is not enough to profess faith in the democratic process; we must do something about it."
> —Ella Grasso

Patriotic Beginnings

Ella Rose Tambussi was born on May 10, 1919, in Windsor Locks, Connecticut. Her parents were working-class people who had recently moved to the

Ella Grasso

U.S. from Italy. Ella was a good student. After graduating from high school, she attended Mount Holyoke College in Massachusetts, and earned her bachelor's degree in 1940. She received a master's degree in 1942. Later that year, Ella married school principal Thomas Grasso. They had two children.

In 1941, the U.S. entered World War II (1939-1945). Thousands of American men and women served in the military in Europe and the Pacific. Although Ella Grasso did not enlist in the armed forces, she worked within the United States to better equip U.S. soldiers overseas. Grasso took a job with the War Manpower Commission as the assistant director of research in Connecticut. The Commission hired and trained civilians (nonmilitary staff) to work in jobs that were important to the war effort, such as making airplanes and weapons, or shipping food to U.S. troops.

In many instances, the Commission helped business owners turn their factories into war production facilities. Often, women were recruited to perform jobs normally held by men, such as welding and assembly-line work. Grasso's department conducted research on where new factories should be built and the number of workers needed.

A Career in Politics

In 1943, Grasso got her first taste of politics when she joined the League of Women Voters and became a speechwriter for the Democratic Party. By 1952, Grasso was writing speeches for her own campaigns, and she was elected to the Connecticut House of Representatives. After serving two two-year terms, she became the Secretary of State in Connecticut in 1958, a position that she held for the next 12 years.

In 1970, Grasso was elected to the U.S. Congress, serving in the House of Representatives. After serving two terms, Grasso set her sights on becoming governor of Connecticut.

Governor of Connecticut

Grasso started campaigning in early 1974 to become governor of Connecticut. In November of that year, she was elected—the first time in U.S. history that a woman was elected as a governor. Before then, several women had served as governors, but none had been elected in their own right. In all those instances, women had served after their governor husbands died in office. Such governorships were considered "inherited." Grasso, however, was elected by the people.

Connecticut citizens voted for Grasso because she believed in the rights of working-class people. She supported women's issues and helped bring the state out of an economic slump. She delivered on her promise to listen to the needs of the people of Connecticut. During an economic crisis, she gave her $7,000 raise back to the state treasury.

Grasso also was known as the champion of minorities, women, young people, and senior citizens. She

---

TOPICAL TIDBIT

Nellie Tayloe Ross

Nellie Tayloe Ross was the first female governor in the United States. She was elected governor of Wyoming in 1924 after her husband—incumbent governor William Bradford Ross—died. She sought reelection in 1926 but lost. In 1933, Ross was appointed director of the U.S. Mint, becoming the first woman to hold such a high federal position.

gained the trust and support of many citizens in Connecticut. She was re-elected in 1978 to serve a second term as governor. In 1980, however, she became ill, and on New Year's Eve 1980, Grasso resigned. She died on February 5, 1981, in Hartford, Connecticut.

A Place in History

Ella Grasso served the people of Connecticut for 28 years. She was trusted by the people of her home state—she never lost an election. In 1993, Grasso was inducted into the National Women's Hall of Fame. A technical school has been named in her memory.

LIFE EVENTS

1919
Ella Rose Tambussi is born in Windsor Locks, Connecticut.

1941
Tambussi works for the War Manpower Commission during World War II.

1942
Ella Tambussi marries Thomas Grasso.

1958-1970
Ella Grasso serves as secretary of state in Connecticut.

1971-1975
Grasso serves as a member of the House of Representatives.

1975-1980
Grasso serves as governor of the state of Connecticut.

1981
Ella Grasso dies in Hartford, Connecticut.

Fannie Lou Hamer
Civil-rights Activist
(born 1917 • died 1977)

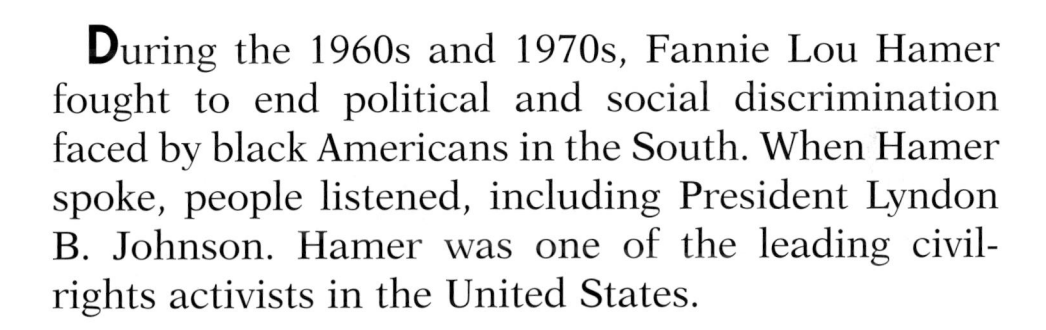

During the 1960s and 1970s, Fannie Lou Hamer fought to end political and social discrimination faced by black Americans in the South. When Hamer spoke, people listened, including President Lyndon B. Johnson. Hamer was one of the leading civil-rights activists in the United States.

Picking Cotton

Fannie Lou Townsend was born on October 6, 1917, in Ruleville, Mississippi. She was the youngest of 20 children. When she was six, Fannie Lou joined the rest of the family picking cotton in the fields of a wealthy plantation owner. The Townsends were sharecroppers, which meant that they worked in the fields planting and harvesting crops for the owner of the plantation.

In return for their work, the Townsends were given a percentage of the profits. Although this may seem like a fair arrangement, it was not. The owner

Fannie Lou Hamer speaks to supporters of the Mississippi Freedom Democratic Party in Washington, D.C., September 17, 1965.

charged the family for the seeds they planted and billed them for using tractors and tools. The owner charged whatever price he wanted, and the Townsends had to pay it. Many sharecroppers never got out of debt, no matter how hard they worked.

Fannie Lou went to school, but dropped out in the sixth grade so she could work full time. In 1944, she married a sharecropper named Perry "Pap" Hamer, and the two began working the land, also as sharecroppers at the Marlow plantation near Ruleville.

Registering to Vote

In 1962, Fannie Lou Hamer had had enough of sharecropping and wanted to gain some control over her life. She went to a meeting of the Student Nonviolent Coordinating Committee (SNCC) to register to vote. SNCC was an organization of young people who held peaceful protests in support of equal rights for blacks. At that time, citizens of southern states had to pass a test to register to vote. The voter-registration tests were designed to keep poor, uneducated people—especially African Americans—from voting.

Hamer took the test. She failed but was deter-

TOPICAL TIDBIT

Murder in Mississippi

In the summer of 1964, civil rights groups sent college students throughout the south to register African Americans to vote. Many students were bullied and beaten. Near Philadelphia, Mississippi, three students—two white and one black—were murdered, bringing about a federal investigation of the Ku Klux Klan, a white hate group.

mined to vote. She studied and took the test again the following month, but failed again. Hamer told the clerk, "You'll see me every 30 days till I pass." In 1963 she passed the test on her third attempt and became a registered voter.

> "I'm sick and tired of being sick and tired."
> —Fannie Lou Hamer

Getting registered to vote was just the first challenge. Blacks who got that far faced more obstacles, such as threats or even attacks by racist whites. News of Hamer's victory reached the Marlow plantation, and the owner fired her.

Hamer began working with SNCC to help other African Americans pass the voting test. When word got out that an African American woman was helping other blacks register to vote, they arrested Hamer and put her in jail. While there, Hamer was beaten so badly that she could not get up. She sustained permanent damage from that beating.

Challenging the Democrats

Hamer became a freedom fighter, seeking civil rights for all African Americans. In 1964, she helped establish the Mississippi Freedom Democratic Party (MFDP). The MFDP wanted to represent Mississippi's Democrats at the 1964 Democratic National Convention in Atlantic City, New Jersey. The MFDP's

◇ Fannie Lou Hamer ◇

members believed that they represented Mississippi better than the all-white delegation from the Democratic Party. Still, the MFDP was not allowed to participate in the presidential nomination process.

An MFDP delegation—64 blacks and 4 whites—went to Atlantic City anyway. When they arrived, they demanded that their members be allowed to replace the official, all-white delegation. They were offered two spots out of the eight given to Mississippi delegates. The MFDP declined, saying that, according to the people of Mississippi, they should have all of the spots.

In a nationally televised speech, Hamer described the unfair treatment of blacks in the south. She talked about voter testing and the brutal beating she had received because she was a black who had registered to vote. Hamer's moving speech got

LIFE EVENTS

1917
Fannie Lou Townsend is born in Ruleville, Mississippi.

1944
Fannie Lou Townsend marries Perry "Pap" Hamer.

1963
After much effort, Fannie Lou Hamer gains her right to vote.

1964
Hamer helps establish the MFDP. She and other delegates travel to Atlantic City, New Jersey, for the Democratic National Convention.

1971
Hamer helps to found the National Women's Political Caucus.

1977
Fannie Lou Hamer dies.

the attention of the American people and of President Johnson. One of the first things Johnson did after the election was to help pass the Voting Rights Act of 1965, and sign it into law. It made it illegal to require voter-registration tests and to deny Americans the right to vote based on the color of their skin.

A Freedom Fighter to the End

Fannie Lou Hamer continued to fight for civil rights until her death on March 14, 1977. In Mississippi she created organizations to help poor African Americans become business owners, land owners, and farmers. She helped establish low-income housing programs, day-care programs, and fought to desegregate schools. She also continued the political fight for blacks and for women, helping establish the National Women's Political Caucus. Fannie Lou Hamer made a huge impact on people—white and black—around the nation.

Audrey Hepburn
Actor and Humanitarian
(born 1929 • died 1993)

A symbol of glamour and grace, Audrey Hepburn dazzled moviegoers with her beautiful clothes, natural grace, and unending charm. She starred in romantic comedies and dramas opposite Hollywood's favorite leading men, including Humphrey Bogart, William Holden, and Gregory Peck. Hepburn also had a heart of gold: She spent many years helping starving children as a goodwill ambassador for UNICEF.

Resisting the Nazis

Edda Kathleen van Heemstra Hepburn-Ruston was born on May 4, 1929, in Brussels, Belgium. She was called Audrey. Her father was an English banker and her mother was a Dutch baroness. Audrey spent her early years in London, England. In 1935, her father left the family.

When World War II broke out in 1939, Audrey's mother thought that the Netherlands would be

◇ 50 American Women ◇

Audrey Hepburn poses with her 1953 Oscar for Best Actress in *Roman Holiday*.

safer than England, so she and Audrey moved there. Unfortunately, the Nazis invaded the Netherlands in 1940. Audrey and her mother were not allowed to leave the country, so they made the best of the situation—Audrey attended school and studied ballet.

Life during the war was horrifying. Audrey's uncle and cousins were shipped off to work camps by the Nazis. Audrey wanted to do what she could to help force the Nazis out of the Netherlands. So she raised money for the Dutch Resistance (Dutch citizens fighting the Nazis) by giving secret dance performances. She also delivered messages between members of the Resistance and people in hiding. She tucked the messages into her shoes, so that the Nazis would not find them. As the war raged on, food was in short supply; Audrey ate tulip bulbs to keep from starving. Malnourishment caused her to grow up very thin. In later years, many people believed that Audrey stayed so thin on purpose, but it was a result of her having been starved during the war.

A Star Is Born

When the Nazis were defeated, Audrey Hepburn and her mother returned to England. Hepburn continued to study ballet in the hopes of becoming a dancer. She also took modeling jobs to earn extra money. That led to small acting parts. In 1951, Hepburn appeared in *The Lavender Hill Mob*, a British movie about bungling bank robbers. Later that year, Colette, a famous French playwright, asked Hepburn to take the lead in her new play, *Gigi*, when it opened on Broadway. Hepburn jumped at the chance.

Next came Hepburn's first starring role, in *Roman Holiday*, for which she won the 1953 Academy Award for Best Actress. Without meaning to, Hepburn's character started a fashion trend. In the film, she portrayed a princess who runs away from her royal duties for a day, cuts her hair short, and is seen wearing an oversized man's shirt with the sleeves rolled up. Soon after the movie premiered, women all over the United States cropped their hair and began wearing men's shirts.

> "For attractive lips, speak words of kindness. For lovely eyes, seek out the good in people. . . . For poise, walk with the knowledge that you'll never walk alone."
>
> —Audrey Hepburn

Hepburn continued to act throughout the 1950s and 1960s in such features as *Sabrina*, *My Fair Lady*, and *Breakfast at Tiffany's*. She also appeared in the film version of Lillian Hellman's *The Children's Hour*.

Hepburn was married twice, first to actor Jose Ferrer, then to psychiatrist Andrea Dotti. She had one child from each marriage: Sean Ferrer and Luca Dotti.

◈ Audrey Hepburn ◈

Feeding the World's Children

Beginning in the 1970s, Hepburn took on a different role—one she considered the most important of her life. Remembering her difficult childhood during the war, Hepburn devoted much of her time raising money to feed hungry children throughout the world.

In 1988, she became a "goodwill ambassador" for the United Nations Children's Fund (UNICEF), a group that raises money to help feed and clothe children in less developed countries, as well as provide them with medical care and education. Hepburn traveled all over the world promoting this cause. She spent the last several years of her life helping to feed starving children in South America and Africa. Hepburn died of colon cancer on January 20, 1993, in Tolochenaz, Switzerland.

TOPICAL TIDBIT

UNICEF

The United Nations International Children's Emergency Fund, commonly called UNICEF, was established in 1946 to help homeless children in the aftermath of World War II (1939-1945). In 1953, its official name changed to the United Nation's Children's Fund. Today, UNICEF supplies food, clothing, education, and health care to children in more than 130 countries. Donations are accepted from private citizens as well as governments.

Quiet Generosity

Audrey Hepburn's work in films and with UNICEF earned her one Academy Award (for *Roman Holiday*), four other Oscar nominations (for *Sabrina*, 1954; *The Nun's Story*, 1959; *The Children's Hour*, 1961; and *Breakfast at Tiffany's*, 1961) and the Jean Hersholt Humanitarian Award from the Academy of Motion Picture Arts and Sciences. Her kindness, elegance, and style had an impact on American culture 30 years ago, and still do today.

LIFE EVENTS

1929
Audrey Hepburn is born in Brussels, Belgium.

1951
Hepburn plays the lead in the Broadway production of *Gigi*.

1953
Hepburn wins the Academy Award for Best Actress for her starring role in *Roman Holiday*.

1961
Hepburn stars in the highly successful film *Breakfast at Tiffany's*.

1988
Hepburn becomes a goodwill ambassador for UNICEF.

1993
Audrey Hepburn dies of colon cancer in Switzerland.

Anne Hutchinson
Champion of Religious Freedom
(born 1591 • died 1643)

One of the founding principles of the United States is that everyone is allowed to worship whatever religion he or she chooses. However, during colonial days, this was not always the case. Anne Hutchinson was someone who suffered because of her beliefs. Her courage helped bring the idea of religious freedom to all Americans.

A Quiet Life

Anne Hutchinson did not seem like the type of person who would cause trouble. She was born Anne Marbury in England in 1591. In 1612, she married a merchant named William Hutchinson. In 1634, the Hutchinsons moved their family to Boston, which—at that time—was a small town in the Massachusetts Bay Colony. Most of the people who lived there were members of a strict religious movement called

◆ 50 American Women ◆

In 1637, Anne Hutchinson was put on trial for her beliefs.

Puritanism. Puritans had many severe rules to follow. They strongly believed that the only true Christians were people who followed all of these rules to the letter.

William Hutchinson had been a rich landowner in England. When he, Anne, and their children moved

◇ Anne Hutchinson ◇

to the American colonies, they soon became one of the most well-known and most popular families in Boston. Anne Hutchinson worked as a midwife, delivering babies, and she had many friends among the women of the town.

Trouble!

Anne Hutchinson was a very religious person. Her father had been a minister, and she had read the Bible and other religious works. She decided to share her views on religious questions with Boston's women, and so began holding meetings in her home. During those meetings, the women discussed what their minister had said in church on Sunday, and what they thought about it. They also talked about how they believed a person should worship God.

During the meetings, Hutchinson told her friends that she believed in a "covenant of grace" from God for each person. (A *covenant* is a formal, solemn, unbreakable promise.) She said that people had to talk to God themselves. They could not rely on what the minister said. Hutchinson also said that going to church was not important. She encouraged people to think for themselves and find their own way to worship God.

The leaders of the Massachusetts Bay Colony got very angry when they heard what Hutchinson was saying. They thought that she was encouraging people to make up their own rules and do whatever they felt was right. Church leaders worried that people would stop listening to them and stop attending services. Soon Hutchinson was in a lot of trouble.

At first, her friends stood by her. One of her strongest supporters was a well-known and respected minister named John Cotton. Later, however, Massachusetts got a new governor, John Winthrop, who hated Hutchinson's ideas. Under pressure from Winthrop, members of the community began to turn against Hutchinson. Finally, even John Cotton said that she was wrong.

Anne Hutchinson refused to change her beliefs so, in 1637, she was put on trial by Governor Winthrop. When Hutchinson said that Winthrop's rules were "against the word of God," she was convicted by the General Court. Winthrop banished Hutchinson—made her leave Massachusetts forever. However, since it was the middle of winter and Hutchinson was expecting a baby, she was allowed to stay in Boston until spring.

> "As I do understand it, laws, commands, rules, and edicts are for those who have not the light which makes plain the pathway. He who has God's grace in his heart cannot go astray."
>
> —Anne Hutchinson

Anne Hutchinson

Freedom—Then a Violent End

Early in 1638, Hutchinson and her family left Boston and moved to the neighboring colony of Rhode Island. Rhode Island had been founded by Roger Williams, who also had been banished from Massachusetts for his religious beliefs. In Rhode Island, Hutchinson was finally able to worship as she pleased.

Some of her friends and supporters joined the Hutchinsons in Rhode Island. Together, they founded the town of Portsmouth. The Hutchinsons lived there for the next four years, until William Hutchinson died in 1642. After that, Anne moved her family to Pelham Bay on Long Island, New York. They lived quietly there, in a small cabin in the wilderness. A few

---

TOPICAL TIDBIT

Mary Barrett Dyer

One of the people who followed Anne Hutchinson to Rhode Island was Mary Barrett Dyer. Like Hutchinson, Dyer strongly believed in religious freedom. Eventually, Dyer became a member of the Society of Friends, also called the Quakers, and returned to Massachusetts to be a Quaker missionary. When Massachusetts passed anti-Quaker laws, Dyer's life was in danger. She was banished twice and almost hanged for her beliefs—but kept going back. Finally, in 1660, she was hanged, but her death made more people see the importance of religious freedom.

months later, in 1643, Hutchinson and her family were attacked by Narragansett Indians, who burned their home, killing everyone except one of Hutchinson's daughters.

Although Anne Hutchinson had been banished from Massachusetts, she was not forgotten there. Today, a statue of her stands on Beacon Hill in Boston. It reminds everyone of this brave woman, who was not afraid to lose everything for what she believed in.

LIFE EVENTS

1591
Anne Marbury is born in England.

1634
Anne and William Hutchinson move their family to the Massachusetts Bay Colony.

1636
Anne Hutchinson comes into conflict with John Winthrop, the governor of Massachusetts.

1637
Winthrop puts Hutchinson on trial for opposing the Puritan ministers. Convicted and banished, Hutchinson moves to the colony of Rhode Island in 1638.

1643
Hutchinson and her family, living on Long Island, are killed by Narragansett Indians.

Mae Jemison
Doctor, Engineer, Astronaut
(born 1956)

When she was young, Mae Jemison knew that she wanted to go into space. She studied hard and became a doctor, then an engineer. Then, in her 30s, Jemison joined NASA and headed into space, proving to the world that dreams can come true. She has continued to work in the sciences by starting several companies devoted to advanced technology. She also encourages youth to get involved in science through educational programs, such as The Earth We Share (TEWS).

Becoming a Scientist

Mae Carol Jemison was born on October 17, 1956, in Decatur, Alabama. She was the youngest of three children and moved to Chicago with her family when she was three years old. During her childhood, she was interested in science, including the study of people (anthropology), the study of civilizations (archaeology), and the study of space (astronomy).

Mae Jemison, at parachute survival school, trained hard to become NASA's first black, female astronaut.

Such subjects were often more appealing to boys than girls. But Mae liked science and decided to make it her career.

When Mae was just 16, she began attending Stanford University, studying African American history and chemical engineering. After graduation in 1977, she went to medical school at Cornell University. While studying to become a doctor, Mae visited several developing nations, including Thailand and Kenya. She offered her medical services to the

◆ Mae Jemison ◆

people who lived there.

Mae Jemison's experiences overseas helped her learn more about the different health problems that affect people in developing nations, and the type of medical care that is needed. After graduation, Jemison worked as a doctor in Los Angeles, California.

> "I believe at the heart of science are the words *I think, I wonder, and I understand.*"
> —Mae Jemison

Joining the Peace Corps

Jemison enjoyed being in L.A., but she wanted to do more. In 1983, she joined the Peace Corps and traveled to Africa. The Peace Corps sends volunteers to developing nations to help local communities construct buildings and bridges, and plant and harvest crops. Some Peace Corps volunteers provide medical assistance and teaching services. Others train local residents in various technologies, so that the citizens can improve their living conditions and learn new skills. In turn, the local residents train others and the community helps itself.

Jemison worked with the Peace Corps in Sierra Leone and Liberia in western Africa. Serving as a medical officer, she provided healthcare services to local people. She also created manuals to help residents learn how to treat common medical problems.

In 1985, she returned to Los Angeles and again worked as a doctor. Her dream to go to space had not died, so Jemison found time to study engineering.

Flying into Space

In the mid-1980s, Jemison applied to the NASA space program, but her first application was rejected. Although she was discouraged, she did not give up. She applied again and was later selected for the program. Jemison was one of 15 people selected from a pool of 2,000 applicants. When Jemison joined the space program in 1987, she became the first African American woman to become an astronaut at NASA.

Training for the astronaut program is demanding, and Jemison rose to the challenge. At NASA, she

---

TOPICAL TIDBIT

Stressing Science

Mae Jemison encourages young people, especially girls and African Americans, to take an interest in the sciences. In previous generations, science was considered a boy's subject, and girls were discouraged from studying math, chemistry, physics, biology, and the like. Mae Jemison has shown that females can make significant contributions in the world of science.

combined her knowledge of medicine and engineering. In September 1992, Jemison again made NASA history when she became the first African American woman to rocket into space. Her dream had come true. Aboard the space shuttle *Endeavor*, Jemison studied gravity's effects on animals and people.

Jemison left NASA in 1993 to pursue other opportunities. She began her own company, the Jemison Group, which works with new and advanced technologies. She also helped to create The Earth We Share (TEWS) international science camp for students.

Jemison also began teaching at Dartmouth College, in Hanover, New Hampshire, and oversaw the Jemison Institute there. The institute worked with developing nations. Jemison has appeared on television in shows such as the *World of Wonder* on the Discovery Channel. She also had a role in an episode of *Star Trek: The Next Generation*.

In 1999, Jemison founded BioSentient, a medical technology corporation. The firm creates mobile medical equipment that monitors people's vital signs to help treat stress, anxiety, and nausea. She has also joined the Bayer Corporation as its national spokesperson. In this role, she talks to people in various communities about the importance of science and education.

Jemison has also written a book for teens about her life, called *Find Where the Wind Goes: Moments from*

My Life. The work was published in 2001. She is also the recipient of many awards. In 2003, Jamison was a Women's History Month honoree with the National Women's History Project. A year later, she joined the board of directors of Gen-Probe, another corporation dedicated to advanced medical technology.

Fulfilling Dreams

Jemison charted new territory by becoming the first black woman in space. She continues to share her knowledge with others, and she serves as a role model to women of all races.

LIFE EVENTS

1956
Mae Carol Jemison is born in Decatur, Alabama.

1977
Jemison graduates from Stanford University.

1983
Jemison joins the Peace Corps.

1992
Jemison becomes the first African American woman to travel in space.

1993
Jemison founds the Jemison Group, Inc.

1999
Jemison establishes BioSentient, a medical technology company.

2004
Gen-Probe selects Jemison to serve on its board of directors.

Mother Jones
(Mary Harris Jones)
Labor Leader
(born 1830 • died 1930)

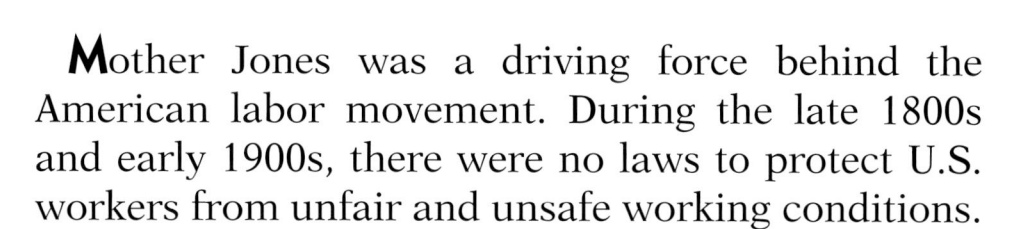

Mother Jones was a driving force behind the American labor movement. During the late 1800s and early 1900s, there were no laws to protect U.S. workers from unfair and unsafe working conditions. Mother Jones and other leaders of labor-reform movements forced big businesses to treat workers fairly.

> "I abide where there is a fight against wrong."
> —Mother Jones

Learning about Unions

Mary Harris was born near Cork, Ireland, on May 1, 1830. When Mary was a young girl, her family moved to Toronto, Canada. Mary went to school and studied to be a teacher.

In 1861, Mary married George Jones. They had four children and lived in Memphis, Tennessee. George was an iron molder who worked in a factory. He worked long hours and received little pay in return. Also, his work was dangerous and there were no safety guidelines. Sometimes, the owners bullied workers by holding back pay. George and many other workers were unhappy with these conditions. George became a trade-union organizer.

A trade union is a group of people who work in a trade—such as iron molding—and join together to demand certain rights from their bosses. Trade unions talk with business owners on behalf of all the employees, for such benefits as fair pay and a safe work environment.

Along with trade unions were labor reformers.

Labor reformers worked to make conditions in all industries better. Reformers wanted to set the maximum number of hours a person could work in a week, set age requirements for child workers, and establish government-sponsored safety boards.

Mary Jones learned a lot by watching George organize his fellow iron molders. It was a dangerous job: Sometimes workers who talked about forming a union were beaten.

Death and Fire

When Mary was 37, tragedy struck her family. George and their four children died during a yellow fever outbreak in 1867. Not knowing what to do, Mary Jones moved to Chicago, Illinois, and opened a dressmaking shop.

Four years later, tragedy stuck again. On October 8, 1871, fire swept through the streets of Chicago. For three days, the city was ablaze; Chicago's business district and many residential areas burned to the ground. More than 250 people died and 90,000 were left homeless. Jones survived, but she lost her home and business.

"Join the Union, Boys!"

After losing everything in the fire, Jones joined the Knights of Labor, a group dedicated to improving working conditions. Known as "Mother Jones," she became a union organizer, following in her husband's footsteps. Her motto was, "Join the union, boys!"

Mother Jones was bold and determined. She helped organize clothing workers, streetcar workers, steel workers, and the United Mine Workers of America (UMWA).

Sometimes, to get business owners to listen to the needs of the workers, the unions would call for a strike. A strike is when workers stop working in protest. Sometimes the factories would close down. Striking workers often gathered outside the factories to raise awareness about why they were striking. Mother Jones would always join them.

Mother Jones led labor reforms as well. She was one of the founders of the International Workers of the World (IWW). Known as the Wobblies, the IWW had members all over the world. Unions in dozens of countries met with business owners to work out better

TOPICAL TIDBIT

March of the Mill Children

In July 1903, Mother Jones marched with a group of children from Philadelphia, Pennsylvania, to President Teddy Roosevelt's home in Oyster Bay, New York. She organized the march to protest unfair child labor practices. Her efforts brought the issue to the attention of President Roosevelt and the entire nation.

wages and working conditions while workers were on strike.

Sometimes, however, emotions flared during a strike and things got violent. The police would come in and arrest the union organizers, striking workers, and business owners for disturbing the peace. When Mother Jones was 89 years old, she was thrown in jail after she joined striking steel-mill workers.

An Inspiration to All

Mother Jones died on November 30, 1930, in Silver Spring, Maryland, at the age of 100. She had helped improve working conditions around the country. In 1984, she was inducted into the National Women's Hall of Fame. *Mother Jones* magazine, dedicated to promoting social change in the world, was named in her honor.

LIFE EVENTS

1830
Mary Harris is born near Cork, Ireland.

1867
Mary Harris Jones loses her husband and four children to yellow fever.

1898
Jones helps found the Social Democratic Party.

1905
Jones helps found the Industrial Workers of the World to promote labor reforms.

1925
Jones publishes her autobiography.

1930
Mother Jones dies in Silver Spring, Maryland.

Helen Keller
Activist for the Disabled
(born 1880 • died 1968)

Unable to see or hear, Helen Keller lived in a world of darkness. She wanted to communicate with others around her, but did not know how. With the help of special teachers, she climbed out of her lonely world and learned to read, write, and speak. Keller showed that a severely impaired person could overcome the limits of her disabilities. She became a strong supporter of the rights of the disabled.

> "Life is either a daring adventure or nothing."
> —Helen Keller

Trapped in Darkness

When Helen Adams Keller was born on June 27, 1880, in Tuscumbia, Alabama, she could see and hear. When she was 19 months old, however, she got sick (perhaps with scarlet fever). The illness destroyed Helen's vision and hearing. Not knowing how to com-

Helen Keller

Annie Sullivan (right) spells out the words of a book into Helen Keller's palm.

municate, Helen often became frustrated as a child. She would throw temper tantrums, kicking and screaming at those around her.

Some people thought that Helen was mentally disabled, too. Her parents knew otherwise. They had seen her try to communicate by touching people's lips and throats as they spoke. Helen could recognize people by touching their faces. She also felt people's hands as they were doing a task, then tried to do it the same way. She had even learned to milk a cow.

Despite her intelligence, Helen was wild. She could not tell people what she liked, disliked, or wanted to do. In her frustration, she would throw and break things, and hurl herself around the house.

When Helen was six, her parents hired a teacher for her. The teacher, Anne Sullivan, had been nearly blind before doctors were able to restore her sight. Sullivan knew the emotional pain of being trapped in darkness.

Amazing Breakthrough

Sullivan's work with Helen Keller was not easy. At first, Keller got angry with Sullivan, even kicked and bit her. Sullivan kept at it, however, and eventually got her pupil to understand sign language. Sullivan would make letters with her fingers that spelled out words. Since Keller could not see the signs, Sullivan spelled the words into the palm of Keller's hands. Keller then created special signs so that she could communicate with her family. She also learned how to read by using braille (patterns of raised dots representing letters).

Keller did not stop there—she learned to speak. She studied with Sarah Fuller, a teacher who helped

Helen Keller

many deaf people learn to speak. Keller learned to make certain sounds, as well as read lips, by touching a speaker's lips and throat.

A successful student, Keller went on to college. She graduated from Radcliffe College in 1904. Sullivan stayed at Keller's side, spelling out the lessons into her pupil's hands. In fact, Sullivan continued to help Keller until the teacher died in 1936.

Helen Keller's Influence

Keller became a writer, using a special typewriter. She wanted to tell the world what it was like to be blind. She wrote magazine articles as well as books. Her first book was an autobiography called *The Story of My Life*. Keller also spoke on behalf of the American Foundation for the Blind, which helped people with vision problems. With the help of an

---

TOPICAL TIDBIT

Super Man, Super Human

The late actor and director Christopher Reeve, best known for playing Superman in a series of popular films, was paralyzed in a horse-riding accident in 1995. Reeve, who used a wheelchair to get around and struggled to speak, became a tireless activist. His work to increase public awareness about physical disabilities reminds people that the disabled are capable of making great contributions to the world.

interpreter, she lectured in the United States, Egypt, South Africa, England, and other countries.

During her lifetime, Keller became interested in equality. She supported women's rights and civil rights, and worked to help the disabled. In her day, many disabled people were sent to mental institutions because their families did not know how to help or teach them. Keller showed that, with proper training, the disabled could lead successful lives.

Helen Keller died on June 1, 1968. During her life, she changed the way that people viewed the disabled. Keller continues to be an inspiration to others. In 1973, she was inducted into the National Women's Hall of Fame. She was also named one of the 100 most influential people of the 20th century by *Time* magazine.

LIFE EVENTS

1880
Helen Adams Keller is born in Tuscumbia, Alabama.

1882
Keller contracts a disease—possibly scarlet fever—that leaves her blind and deaf.

1886
The Keller family hires Anne Sullivan to be Helen's teacher.

1903
Keller's autobiography, *The Story of My Life*, is published.

1904
With the help of Sullivan, Keller graduates from Radcliffe College.

1968
Helen Keller dies.

Billie Jean King
Tennis Champion
(born 1943)

Armed with a tennis racket, Billie Jean King scored a huge victory for female athletes when she defeated male tennis pro Bobby Riggs in 1973. The highly publicized match, dubbed the "battle of the sexes," showed the world that female athletes are just as skilled and capable as male athletes. That was just one of many important victories for King throughout her career.

Finding Her Way

Billie Jean Moffitt was born on November 22, 1943, in Long Beach, California. She showed an interest in sports at an early age and was a talented softball player. Her parents thought that tennis would be a better sport for her because it was more "ladylike." So Billie Jean took up tennis.

Billie Jean had a natural ability in tennis, and she had the determination to succeed. In 1961, at 17, Billie Jean competed at Wimbledon in England—one

Billie Jean King goes for a shot during the opening match of the San Francisco tennis tournament in 1974.

of the largest tennis competitions in the world. Billie Jean and her teammate, Karen Hantz, won the doubles championship that year.

In 1965, Billie Jean Moffitt married Larry King. (They have since divorced.) Billie Jean King kept winning tennis tournaments. In the 1960s and 1970s, she earned 20 Wimbledon titles, in both individual and doubles contests. She also participated in—and won—other major contests, including the U.S. Open, the French Open, and the Australian Open. She became one of the most successful female tennis players the world has ever seen. In 1967, she won the singles, doubles, and mixed doubles titles in the United States and at Wimbledon. She was the first woman to do this since Alice Marble in the late 1930s.

> "I think self-awareness is probably the most important thing toward being a champion."
> —Billie Jean King

Paving the Way

King's achievements had a much greater impact on sports than her athletic skill, alone, had. She made it acceptable for girls to get more involved in sports. Before then, many girls were discouraged from participating in sports that required a lot of physical effort. Such activities were considered "boyish." King ignored that, however, and led the way for other girls to follow.

King made history in 1971 when she became the first female athlete to earn more than $100,000 in a single year. Despite her successes, she often spoke out about the inequality between men and women in tennis. Up until this point, female athletes got paid less than male athletes for winning the same tournaments. King urged contest sponsors to offer equal prize money to male and female athletes. When she won on the U.S. Open in 1972, she received $15,000 less than the male winner did. As a result, she refused to participate in the contest in 1973 unless the prizes were equal. The sponsors of the U.S. Open honored the request.

Billie Jean King's outspoken demands for equality in tennis came to the attention of player Bobby Riggs, and he challenged her to a match. He claimed that a woman could not beat him, even if he was 55 and she was 29. He admitted that he was a male chauvinist—that is, he truly believed that men were much more capable than women. He kept on challenging King until she agreed to meet him on the tennis court. Millions of television viewers watched as she proved him wrong in September of 1973. In what is probably the most-watched tennis match in history, Billie Jean King beat Bobby Riggs by a score of 6-4, 6-3, 6-3.

TOPICAL TIDBIT

Tennis Before Mass

The game of tennis began hundreds of years ago. Historians trace its origins back to monks who played the game in monasteries—the religious centers where they lived, worked, and prayed. Apparently monks enjoyed the game so much that some church officials outlawed tennis at monasteries in 1245.

No Stopping Billie Jean

King continued to help female tennis players by co-founding the Women's Tennis Association in 1974. She also helped establish World Team Tennis with Larry King, her ex-husband. Her other contributions are numerous, including founding the Women's Sports Foundation and *WomenSports* magazine. She has also found time to work with children who cannot afford to pay for tennis lessons.

King's awards and honors include induction into the International Tennis Hall of Fame and the Women's Sports Hall of Fame. In 1990, she was also inducted into the National Women's Hall of Fame. *Life* magazine named her one of the 100 most important Americans in the 20th century, and she continues to be involved in tennis as a coach and a commentator. She has lent her talents to sports shows on ABC, CBS, NBC, HBO, and other networks.

King coached the U.S. Olympic Women's Tennis Team in 1996 and 2000. She has written several books, including, in 1988, *We Have Come a Long Way: The History of Women's Tennis*. She also serves on the board of directors for the Elton John AIDS Foundation and the National AIDS Fund. In 2006, through Billie Jean King WTT Charities, she offered scholarships to student tennis players with diabetes. Her foundation began helping diabetic students in 1998.

In 2003, she became one of the first players to be

inducted into the U.S. Open Court of Champions. She shared that honor with players such as Chris Evert and Jimmy Connors. That same year, she received the International Tennis Federation's Philippe Chatrier Award.

Billie Jean King rose to the top of her profession when she was just a teenager. She worked hard to demonstrate that women athletes are just as talented as men are. She opened the door for the many female athletes—in tennis and other sports—who have followed her inspiring example.

LIFE EVENTS

1943
Billie Jean Moffitt is born in California.

1971
King becomes the first woman in tennis to earn more than $100,00 in a year.

1972
King wins the U.S. Open and refuses to return unless the women's prizes are equal to the men's.

1973
King beats Bobby Riggs in the "Battle of the Sexes" match.

1974
King co-founds the Women's Tennis Association.

1996, 2000
King coaches U.S. Olympic Women's Tennis Team.

Maggie Kuhn
Advocate for the Elderly
(born 1905 • died 1995)

For most of her life, Maggie Kuhn led a quiet, normal existence. However, when she was 65 years old, she began the most important work of her life: winning equal rights for the elderly.

A Political Family

Maggie Kuhn's parents lived in Memphis, Tennessee. They were white, but Maggie's mother hated the segregation laws in Memphis so much that she didn't want her daughter to be born there. So Mrs. Kuhn traveled to Buffalo, New York, to stay with her parents, where Margaret Eliza Kuhn was born on August 3, 1905.

The Kuhns later returned to Memphis. When Maggie was a teenager, the family moved to Cleveland, Ohio. Maggie enrolled at Case Western Reserve University in Cleveland to study English and sociology.

Along with her parents' hatred of segregation, members of the family also worked to win voting rights for women. Maggie shared her family's interest in making things better for all people. During her years at Case Western Reserve, she helped start a campus chapter of the League of Women Voters, an organization that supports the right and responsibility of all people to vote.

A Working Woman

After graduating from college in 1926, Kuhn began working at the Cleveland YWCA. Her job included setting up programs for young working women. As Kuhn talked with these women, she discovered that they worked long hours in offices and factories, but received little pay. This made her angry, so she dedicated her life to helping people who were treated unfairly.

During the 1930s, Kuhn moved to New York City, where she continued to work for the YWCA. Then, in 1945, she accepted a job with the United Presbyterian Church. Kuhn coordinated many church activities, including programs on women's rights, racism, and discrimination against the elderly. She also wrote articles for the church's magazine and was an observer at the United Nations.

Kuhn worked for the United Presbyterian Church for 25 years. She loved her job and was very good at it. However, in 1970, when she turned 65, she was forced to retire. Like many organizations at that time, the church had a rule that no one over age 65 could work there.

> "Old age is not a disease—it is strength and survivorship, triumph over all kinds of . . . disappointments, trials, and illnesses."
> —Maggie Kuhn

Fighting Back

Kuhn was furious at having to quit a job she loved. She knew that she was not too old to work, even if society said otherwise. "If you are not prepared, retirement at 65 makes you a nonperson," she said. "It deprives you of the sense of community that has previously defined your life."

Kuhn decided to fight back. In 1971, she and six retired friends formed a group to fight against age discrimination. The group started meeting in a church basement in Philadelphia, Pennsylvania. Kuhn and her friends called themselves the Consultation of Older and Younger Adults for Social Change. The organization grew and started to become more widely known. Because most of the members were elderly, one television reporter referred to them as the Gray Panthers. The name stuck, and soon Kuhn and her Gray Panthers were famous around the country.

The Gray Panthers

From the start, Maggie Kuhn was the organization's leader and its most outspoken member. She wanted everyone to realize that being old did not make a person stupid, helpless, or inferior. Her message was that older people had to take control of their lives and work actively for causes in which they believed. She believed that the elderly are in a

◇ Maggie Kuhn ◇

unique position to create change. "We who are old have nothing to lose!" she wrote. "We have everything to gain by living dangerously! We can initiate [start] change without jeopardizing jobs or family. We can be the risk-takers."

Although the Gray Panthers were focused on the rights of the elderly, the group also had younger members. Most of all, Kuhn wanted to bridge the gap between young and old, and show people of all ages how they could work together to solve social problems. The group also tackled many such problems as the abuse of people living in nursing homes, negative images of the elderly on television, and the lack of public transportation for the handicapped. Into the 1990s,

TOPICAL TIDBIT

The Gray Panthers

Maggie Kuhn's group, the Consultation of Older and Younger Adults for Social Change, was truly a daring organization when it began in 1971. The name was not very catchy, however. The reporter who dubbed them the "Gray Panthers" solved that problem—everyone remembered it after that! He was comparing Kuhn's group to a radical black-power group of the 1960s called the Black Panthers. The Black Panthers were controversial because they had guns and spoke of violence as a way to achieve their goals. Maggie Kuhn and her elderly comrades were not about to use violence, but their ideas were as radical in their way.

the Gray Panthers fought for a national health-care system and a clean environment.

Kuhn remained active in the Gray Panthers until her death on April 22, 1995, at 89. She had asked that her gravestone be inscribed with these words: "Here lies Maggie Kuhn, under the only stone she left unturned."

Through her hard work and dedication, Maggie Kuhn helped many people realize that old age does not have to mean an end to an active life. Instead, it is a time when a person can achieve his or her deepest dreams and help make the world a better place.

LIFE EVENTS

1905
Margaret Eliza Kuhn is born in Buffalo, New York.

1926
Maggie Kuhn begins work at the YWCA in Cleveland, Ohio, and learns of the poor working conditions of young women.

1945
Kuhn begins work for the United Presbyterian Church in New York.

1970
On reaching age 65, Kuhn is forced to retire.

1971
Kuhn and others start an organization, dubbed the Gray Panthers, to fight age discrimination and other problems.

1995
Maggie Kuhn dies at age 89.

Maya Lin
Architect and Artist
(born 1959)

When she was just a 21-year-old Yale University student, Maya Lin entered a national contest to design a memorial for veterans of the Vietnam War. Lin's design beat out more than 1,400 other designs, including those submitted by professional artists and architects. Since then, Maya Lin has designed houses, sculptures, and other memorials. She is among the most successful artists today.

Combining Art and Architecture

Born October 5, 1959, in Athens, Ohio, Maya is the daughter of Henry H. and Julia Lin. Her parents fled from communist China in 1948 to seek freedom in the United States.

Although Maya is of Chinese descent, her parents encouraged her to live an American lifestyle. Both of her parents were professors at the University of Ohio. Her father taught art; her mother taught literature. Both taught Maya to appreciate nature, art, and books.

Maya, who was a very bright child, went on to pursue architecture at Yale University. She also studied sculpture. To her, it was natural to combine those two fields of study. While at Yale, she took a course in funeral architecture, and her professor encouraged the class to enter a national competition to design a memorial that would honor U.S. veterans of the Vietnam War.

Vietnam

In 1961, the U.S. became involved in a civil war between North and South Vietnam in southeast Asia. The U.S. supported the South Vietnamese, who were trying to prevent the communist North Vietnamese from taking control. The involvement of the U.S. in the war bitterly divided Americans. Thousands of young Americans lost their lives in what many Americans saw as another country's problem. Many people held protest marches and rallies. Yet many other Americans supported the war effort. The war lasted until 1975, and 58,000 Americans were killed.

TOPICAL TIDBIT

Impressions of the Wall

People are often overwhelmed when they visit the enormous wall and see the seemingly endless list of names. Names are still being added today as more facts are uncovered. Some people leave items at the Wall, such as photos, flowers, and flags, to honor the memory of their loved ones.

When the soldiers returned from the war, many were treated harshly. It seemed that the American people blamed the soldiers for losing the war.

Over the years, a growing number of people realized that Vietnam veterans had been treated unfairly. In 1980, a committee was assembled to plan the building of a memorial to those who had died in Vietnam or remained missing in action. The committee held a competition to choose the design for the memorial.

"The Wall"

Twenty-one-year-old Maya Lin went to Washington, D.C., to see the site of the memorial. She picked her theme—one that incorporated the natural landscape of the area. Her proposal featured two long walls of polished black granite, in a V-shape, on which the names of the nearly 58,000 men and women killed in Vietnam would be carved. The wall would consist of 150 panels, each 40 inches wide. Each panel would

> "Some people wanted me to put the names in alphabetical order. I wanted them in chronological order so that a veteran could find his time within the panel. It's like a thread of life."
>
> —Maya Lin, on the Vietnam Veterans Memorial

have lines and lines of names.

Lin was one of more than 1,400 people to submit designs to the competition. Coming up with the right design was a challenge because the Vietnam War had so divided the country. During the judging, the contestants' names were withheld so that no committee member would know the identity of the artist until after they had voted. Lin's design was chosen by all the judges. Many were amazed to find out that the winner was a young, female student of Asian descent.

The Controversy

Some veterans and politicians did not like Lin's design because it was different. It did not contain the more traditional elements of a memorial, such as statues of men in uniform. Some critics called it a "scar in the earth." They

LIFE EVENTS

1959
Maya Lin is born in Athens, Ohio.

1981
A committee in Washington, D.C., chooses Lin's design for the Vietnam Veterans Memorial. Lin graduates from Yale University.

1982
The Vietnam Veterans Memorial opens.

1986
Lin gets her master's degree in architecture and opens her own design studio.

1989
Lin designs the Civil Rights Memorial in Montgomery, Alabama.

1993
Lin designs the Women's Table at Yale University.

criticized the judges for picking a design drawn by a woman. Others objected to Lin's youth and Asian heritage.

Lin refused to alter her vision, and the Vietnam Veterans Memorial—sometimes called the Wall—was built in 1982. To calm protesters, two more monuments, one featuring men and another featuring women, were placed near the Wall. Regardless of the controversy, people were deeply moved by the Wall. The impressive monument is now the most visited memorial in the country.

Carving Out a Place for History

Lin went on to get a master's degree and open her own design studio. She has designed more monuments, including a civil-rights memorial in Montgomery, Alabama. The Civil Rights Memorial features water pouring over a granite table listing the names of people killed during the civil-rights movement. It includes a quote by Dr. Martin Luther King Jr.

Lin has also designed a women's monument at Yale University, the Langston Hughes Library in Tennessee, houses, sculpture, and furniture. She continues to combine her love of art and architecture in new and different ways.

Belva Lockwood
Lawyer and Women's Rights Activist
(born 1830 • died 1917)

Women have been fighting for basic rights in the United States since the 1840s. Susan B. Anthony and Elizabeth Cady Stanton led the crusade for women's right to vote. Others paved the way for women to enter professions dominated by men. Belva Lockwood was the first female lawyer allowed to try a case before the U.S. Supreme Court. She helped open the legal profession to women.

The Road to Washington

Belva Ann Bennett was born in Royalton, New York, on October 24, 1830. She grew up on a farm and attended a country school in Niagara County, New York. Belva, who was very intelligent, finished school early. She began teaching when she was just 15 years old.

In addition to teaching, Belva continued her studies

and graduated from Genesee College (now called Syracuse University) in 1857. After meeting Susan B. Anthony—one of the leaders of the women's suffrage movement—Belva realized how important it was for women to have rights equal to men's in the eyes of the law. The more she fought for women's rights, the more she wanted to study law.

Belva Lockwood

Practicing Law

In 1866, Belva moved to Washington, D.C., where she opened a private school. In 1868, she married Ezekiel Lockwood, a minister and dentist. He helped run the school so that Belva could study law.

Belva Lockwood, now in her 40s, applied to some of the best law schools in the country. At first, she was refused because she was a woman. She kept trying, however, and was finally accepted into the law program at National University Law School in Washington. She earned her degree in 1873, then was admitted to the bar in the District of Columbia. At that time, however, the U.S. Supreme Court would not let her try cases because of "custom"—the Court recognized only men as lawyers.

> "The general effect of attempting things beyond us, even though we fail, is to enlarge and liberalize the mind."
> —Belva Lockwood

Lockwood was outraged that the U.S. legal system discriminated against women. She also was concerned by the economic status of women, who were not allowed to own businesses or run households on their own. They needed their husband's permission to make transactions in real estate and finance. Business matters had to be conducted in the courts, yet women were not allowed to be part of the legal system. Lockwood thought that this was unjust, so she took it upon herself to change it.

First, Lockwood drafted a bill that required the U.S. government to pay female employees the same salaries as men who performed similar jobs. The bill passed in 1872. Next, Lockwood submitted a bill to Congress that would grant women the right to practice law before the U.S. Supreme Court. She spent five years lobbying for support. Eventually, the bill was passed. In 1879, Lockwood became the first woman allowed to try cases before the U.S. Supreme Court.

The Crusade for Women's Rights

Lockwood then turned her talents to woman's suffrage. Women had been demanding the right to vote since the 1840s, but each time a bill was submitted to Congress, it failed. Hoping to correct this situation,

TOPICAL TIDBIT

Married Women's Property Acts

Ellen S. Mussey and Belva Lockwood pushed a series of bills through Congress granting women the right to own and profit from businesses. They argued that women made business decisions while their husbands were away, so the government should not keep women from profiting from the decisions they made. The bills were passed into law, known as the Married Women's Property Acts, beginning in 1839.

Belva Lockwood

Lockwood ran for president of the U.S. in 1884. She received more than 4,000 votes, but Grover Cleveland won with more than four million votes.

In 1903, Lockwood wrote amendments to the state constitutions of Arizona, Oklahoma, and New Mexico. These amendments gave women the right to vote in those states.

Fighting until the end, Lockwood died on May 19, 1917. Just three years later, in August 1920, the 19th Amendment to the U.S. Constitution was passed. It granted women the right to vote on a national level.

A Champion of the Law

Belva Lockwood is known as a champion of women's rights, especially in the legal system. She helped make it possible for women to have careers in law. In 1983, Lockwood was inducted into the National Women's Hall of Fame.

LIFE EVENTS

1830
Belva Ann Bennett is born in Royalton, New York.

1872
Belva Lockwood writes a bill requiring equal salaries for men and women doing the same work.

1873
Lockwood gets her law degree.

1879
Lockwood becomes the first woman to try a case in front of the U.S. Supreme Court.

1884
Lockwood unsuccessfully runs for president.

1917
Lockwood dies.

1920
The 19th Amendment is passed, giving U.S. women the right to vote.

Margaret Mead
Anthropologist
(born 1901 • died 1978)

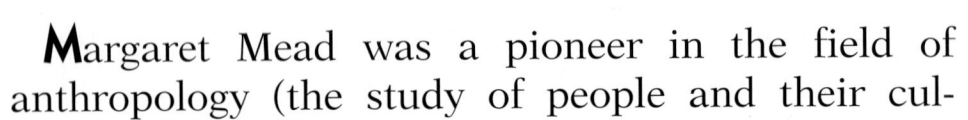

Margaret Mead was a pioneer in the field of anthropology (the study of people and their cultures). Anthropology first came on the scene in the early 1900s as people began to travel farther from home. As they traveled, they encountered new cultures—some similar to theirs, some very different. Margaret Mead dedicated her life to learning about new peoples and then using her wisdom to educate the world.

> "Never doubt that a small group of thoughtful, committed citizens can change the world."
> —Margaret Mead

A New Scientist

Margaret Mead was born on December 16, 1901. She was the first baby born in the newly opened West Park Hospital in Philadelphia, Pennsylvania.

Margaret Mead

Margaret Mead holds a baby of the Manus Tribe, in Papua New Guinea, 1954.

Margaret was the daughter of Edward, a college professor, and Emily, a women's rights activist. The Mead family moved quite often between Pennsylvania, New York, and New Jersey. At times, Margaret went to school; other times, she learned at home.

Margaret went on to Barnard College in New York, and then received her doctorate degree from Columbia University. It was at Barnard that she developed her passion for anthropology.

Studying the Pacific Islanders

In 1925, at just 23 years old, Margaret Mead traveled 2,500 miles to American Samoa, a remote island in the South Pacific Ocean. She went there to study the culture of the Samoan people, who lived quite primitively. They hunted for food, had no electricity or running water, and were unaware of the technological changes going on outside their island nation.

In Samoa, Mead focused on adolescent girls going through puberty. She recognized that the girls in Samoa went through a difficult time in their early teens, just like girls in the U.S. Mead was fascinated to observe that young Samoan women struggled to find their place in society just as young women in America did—despite the vast differences in the two cultures.

A few years later, Mead traveled to the nearby nation of Papua New Guinea. There she further studied the impact that gender had on a person's place in society. She noted how young people can be shaped by the society in which they live. For example, treating girls as inferior is not something that children do automatically. The society in which the children live teaches them how to treat the people around them.

Mead observed this fact firsthand. She studied three different local cultures and observed that, in one group, men and women were equals. They hunted for food together and raised children together.

In another group, males were clearly the superior group. From birth, boys were taught to be aggressive and act superior to girls. It went so far as infanticide—unwanted baby girls were sometimes left to die.

In the third group, women were more aggressive than men. The men raised the children and took care of the household duties, while the women went in search of food.

TOPICAL TIDBIT

American Museum of Natural History

The American Museum of Natural History houses one of the world's finest collections of plants, animals, and fossils. Located in New York City, the museum was founded in 1869. It was one of the first museums to include exhibits on native cultures throughout the world—an effort largely pushed by Margaret Mead.

Mead compiled her observations into many books, including *Coming of Age in Samoa* and *Growing Up in New Guinea*.

Mead's Influence on Anthropology

In 1926, Mead took a job as an assistant curator at the American Museum of Natural History in New York City. Mead established herself as a driving force in the field of anthropology. By 1964, she was a curator at the museum and headed the division on race and culture. She established the museum's Hall of Pacific Peoples and contributed most of the artifacts on display. That exhibit would not exist if it were not for Margaret Mead.

Throughout her career, Mead taught at colleges and universities. In 1973, she was elected president of the

---

LIFE EVENTS

1901
Margaret Mead is born in Philadelphia, Pennsylvania.

1925
Mead travels to American Samoa.

1926
Mead becomes an assistant curator at the American Museum of Natural History in New York.

1929
Mead travels to Papua New Guinea.

1964
Mead becomes a curator at the museum.

1973
Mead is named president of the American Association for the Advancement of Science.

1978
Margaret Mead dies.

American Association for the Advancement of Science. Mead was also very outspoken on women's rights issues, as well as such topics as nuclear war, drug abuse, and world hunger.

In 1976, Margaret Mead was inducted into the National Women's Hall of Fame. She died on November 15, 1978, in New York City. After her death, she was awarded the Presidential Medal of Freedom, one of the highest honors given in the United States. Mead's work in the field of anthropology will leave a lasting impression on anyone interested in other cultures.

Toni Morrison
Author and Teacher
(born 1931)

In such novels as *Beloved, Jazz,* and *Song of Solomon,* author Toni Morrison explores issues of race and gender in America. She fills her books with keen observations about the lives that African Americans and women have led in a country filled with racial and gender inequality. Morrison has won many writing awards, including the Nobel Prize for Literature.

Growing up in Ohio

Toni Morrison was born Chloe Anthony Wofford on February 18, 1931, in Lorain, Ohio. She was one of four children. Before Morrison was born, her family lived in the South, where racism and discrimination were rampant. It was also the time of the Great Depression, when unemploy-

> "The purpose of freedom is to free someone else."
> —Toni Morrison

Toni Morrison with a copy of her novel *Beloved*, when it was first released in 1987.

ment and homelessness were high, food was scarce, and the entire nation fell on hard times. The Woffords moved north in search of a better life.

During this time, many schools in the United States were segregated. This meant that white students went to different schools than black students. Morrison, however, went to a school with both white and black children.

For a time, Morrison was the only black child in

her class. At first, she did not feel discrimination toward her. As she got older, however, she saw the ways in which blacks were treated differently.

An Interest in Writing

Early in her life, Morrison showed an interest in reading. She loved novels by Leo Tolstoy, Gustave Flaubert, and Jane Austen. Later, she became interested in writing herself. After graduating from high school, she earned a bachelor's degree at Howard University in Washington, D.C., then received her master's degree from Cornell University in Ithaca, New York. While in college, she shortened her name to Toni (from her middle name, Anthony) because some people had difficulty pronouncing her first name, Chloe (KLOH-ee).

After graduation, Morrison began a career as a teacher at Texas Southern University. After that, she joined the faculty of Howard University. There, she met Harold Morrison and the couple married in 1958. They had two sons. However, she was unhappy in her married life.

In 1964, the couple divorced, and Morrison took her sons back to Ohio. She got a job as an associate editor with Random House publishers and joined a writers' group. She wrote a short story for this group that became the key to her second career.

Finding Fame

In 1967, Random House transferred Morrison to New York, where she became a senior editor. She also took her short story and developed it into a novel, called *The Bluest Eye*. The book was published in 1970 to critical acclaim. *The Bluest Eye* is based on a girl Morrison once knew who had struggled to deal with the image of beauty in America—an image that was usually based on white features and characteristics. Seeking to be beautiful, the black character wants to have blue eyes. Morrison followed with more novels, all of which were praised by critics, including *Sula* (1973), *Song of Solomon* (1977), *Tar Baby* (1981), and *Beloved* (1987). Morrison's characters experience and fight discrimination. She writes of prejudice against women and African Americans. In *Beloved*, Morrison tells the story of a slave who escapes, only to be caught and returned to her owner. The slave

TOPICAL TIDBIT

From Page to Screen

In 1998, actor and talk-show host Oprah Winfrey produced and acted in a screen adaptation of Toni Morrison's Pulitzer Prize-winning novel *Beloved*. Winfrey portrays Sethe, a former slave who is haunted by the ghost of her daughter, Beloved.

Toni Morrison receives the 1993 Nobel Prize for Literature, in Stockholm, Sweden.

takes desperate measures rather than have her children face a life of slavery.

Morrison's Mark

In 1993, Morrison made history by becoming only the eighth woman—and first African American woman—to win the Nobel Prize for Literature. Since then she has published *Jazz* (1992), *Paradise* (1998), and *Love* (2003). In 2000, Morrison was honored with the National Humanities Medal. Her book *Remember: The Journey to School Integration* (2004) earned her the Coretta Scott King Award from the American Library Association in 2005.

Morrison has also found time to write children's books with her son, Slade Morrison. These stories include *The Big Box* (2002); *The Book of Mean People* (2002); the *Who's Got Game?* series: *The Lion or the Mouse?*, *The Ant or the Grasshopper?* (both 2003), and *Poppy or the Snake?* (2004); and *The Mirror or the Glass?* (to be released in 2007). In addition, she wrote the libretto for the opera *Margaret Garner*, which was performed in 2005.

Morrison also enjoys teaching. She has said that she takes teaching just as seriously as she does writing. She has held posts at Rutgers University, the State University of New York at Albany, and Princeton University.

Today, Toni Morrison is one of America's most popular and successful writers. A gifted storyteller, she presents characters who struggle to find themselves and maintain their identities in a world full of racial and gender prejudice. Readers recognize the strength and value of her stories.

LIFE EVENTS

1931
Chloe Anthony Wofford is born in Lorain, Ohio.

1953
Toni graduates from Howard University.

1964
Toni becomes an editor for Random House.

1988
Morrison's, *Beloved*, wins the Pulitzer Prize for fiction.

1993
Morrison becomes the first African American woman to win a Nobel Prize for Literature.

2000
Morrison wins the National Humanities Medal.

2005
Morrison wins the Coretta Scott King Award for *Remember*.

Ellen Ochoa
First Hispanic American Woman in Space
(born 1958)

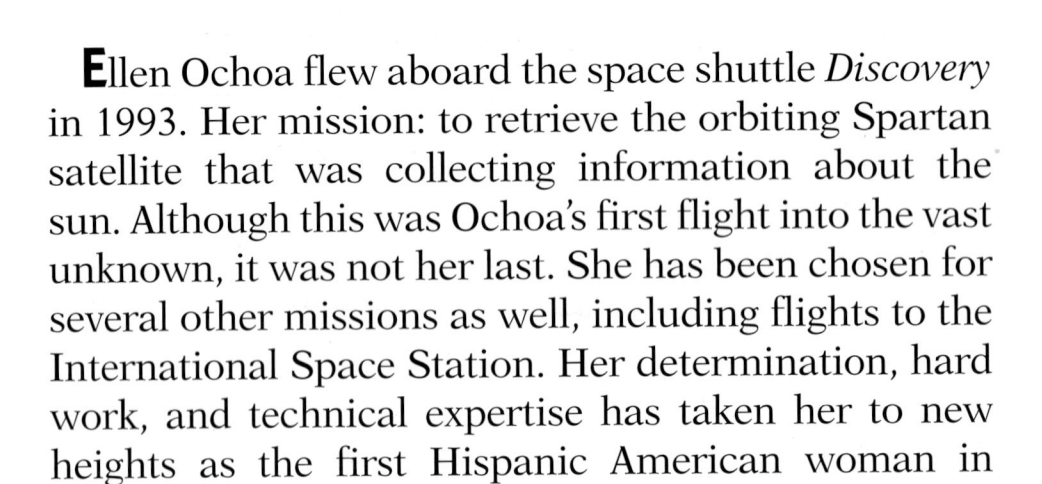

Ellen Ochoa flew aboard the space shuttle *Discovery* in 1993. Her mission: to retrieve the orbiting Spartan satellite that was collecting information about the sun. Although this was Ochoa's first flight into the vast unknown, it was not her last. She has been chosen for several other missions as well, including flights to the International Space Station. Her determination, hard work, and technical expertise has taken her to new heights as the first Hispanic American woman in space.

Early Years

Ellen Ochoa was born in Los Angeles, California, on May 10, 1958. The middle child of five, she had a keen

> "I always liked school, and being an astronaut allows you to learn continuously, like you do in school."
> —Ellen Ochoa

Ellen Ochoa

interest in science and space exploration. However, when Ellen was young, women were not accepted into the astronaut program. So, she pursued other interests, like volleyball and bicycling. She also enjoyed playing the flute.

After Ellen graduated from high school in 1975, she began taking classes at San Diego State University in southern California. She thought about continuing her classical training in music but also considered taking business classes. She was also very gifted in math and the sciences. Eventually, physics won out. She received her Bachelor of Science degree in 1980 and eventually received her doctorate in electrical engineering from Stanford University.

It wasn't until Ellen was in graduate school that she learned that NASA (National Aeronautics and Space Administration) was looking for people with a well-rounded education. Also, by then, NASA was recruiting women for the space program.

> "If you are motivated to excel in one area, you are usually motivated to excel in others. NASA looks for that."
> —Ellen Ochoa

Years Before NASA

Ochoa found her niche as an engineer. She applied for a U.S. patent for one of her inventions. A patent is granted by the government to someone who invents something new. In Ochoa's case, her patent was for an optical information system—a way for computers to determine certain characteristics about an object by looking at it. For example, by using an optical device, such as a camera, the computer program can convert the image to a digital code. The computer program can then "see" certain things that are not visible to the human eye, such as patterns. Ochoa's invention is used for inspecting the quality of manufactured goods.

Ochoa accepted a position at Sandia National Laboratories, a research company that works with the U.S. government on many projects. Through Sandia, Ochoa worked with NASA's Ames Research Center to develop more elaborate optical information systems. Specifically, Ochoa began working in the field of space robotics—using robots to do things that humans cannot do. In order for the robots to do their work, someone (or something such as a computer) has to guide them. Ochoa's work on robotic guidance systems earned her two more patents.

Robots in Space

Ellen Ochoa's work with robotic guidance systems made her a perfect candidate for NASA's astronaut program. On April 4, 1993, the space shuttle

TOPICAL TIDBIT

International Space Station

The International Space Station (ISS) is a laboratory in orbit 200 miles above Earth. Launched in 1998, the ISS conducts research into space exploration as well as in the fields of technology and medicine. Teams from 16 countries worked together to build the ISS. The station is powered by large solar arrays (similar to satellite dishes) that gather energy from the sun and turn it into electricity.
Since November 2000, the ISS has been staffed continuously by members of the U.S. and Russian space programs. Arriving by way of a space shuttle, the three-person crew lives onsite; duty rotations usually last for four to six months.

Discovery left the launch pad with Ochoa aboard. Not only was this her first mission in space, but Ochoa was also the first Hispanic American woman to leave Earth's atmosphere. The *Discovery* crew's 14-day mission was to retrieve the Spartan satellite, which was collecting information about the sun. By guiding the robotic arms attached to the *Discovery*, Ochoa grabbed the satellite from space. Once back on Earth, NASA scientists used the information from Spartan to study the sun's effects on Earth's weather.

Over the next decade, Ochoa flew on three more missions, logging in more than 975 hours in space. In addition to retrieving satellites, Ochoa was also responsible for using the robotic equipment to deliver food, clothes, medical supplies, and other equipment to the International Space Station. She has served at NASA in many areas, including that of mission specialist, flight engineer, and COMCAP—spacecraft communicator for Mission Control. She is currently the deputy director of Flight Crew Operations.

Awards and Rewards

Ochoa is a natural when it comes to space exploration. Her knowledge of computers, engineering, robotics, and space led her to new horizons. It has also allowed her to do things that most people can only dream of, including playing the flute in space.

Through hard work, courage, and determination, Ochoa has opened doors for other women in the field. She has received numerous honors, including the Women in Aerospace Outstanding Achievement Award, the Hispanic Heritage Leadership Award, and NASA's Outstanding Leadership Medal. She was asked to participate in President Bill Clinton's Presidential Commission on the Celebration of Women in American History.

Ellen Ochoa credits her mother as her inspiration. Roseanne Ochoa taught her daughter that learning for the sake of learning was truly reward in and of itself. It is this message that Ochoa hopes young people of today will take to heart.

LIFE EVENTS

1958
Ellen Ochoa is born in Los Angeles, CA.

1993
Ochoa becomes the first Hispanic American woman in space.

1995
NASA awards Ochoa with the Outstanding Leadership Medal.

1999
Ochoa and the crew of *Discovery* dock with the ISS to deliver supplies.

1999
Ochoa is appointed to serve on the Presidential Commission on the Celebration of Women in American History.

2002
Ochoa returns to the ISS to assist in the building of space-walk structures.

Sandra Day O'Connor
U.S. Supreme Court Justice
(born 1930)

Women in the U.S. have struggled and fought for equal rights since the 1840s. Susan B. Anthony and Elizabeth Cady Stanton led the fight for women's suffrage. In 1879, Belva Lockwood became the first female lawyer to try a case before the U.S. Supreme Court. More than 100 years later, in 1981, Sandra Day O'Connor became the first woman to serve as a justice on the Supreme Court of the United States.

> "The power I exert on the court depends on the power of my arguments, not on my gender."
> —Sandra Day O'Connor

Cattle Ranching in Arizona

Sandra Day was born in El Paso, Texas, on March 26, 1930. Her parents, Harry and Ada Mae Day,

◇ Sandra Day O'Connor ◇

owned a 155,000-acre cattle ranch in Arizona, where Sandra grew up. Sandra liked to go horseback riding and play tennis. She also helped out on the ranch, tending to the cattle. Since there were no schools nearby, she attended Radford School in El Paso, a boarding school for girls.

Sandra was an excellent student who studied very hard. Because of her good grades, she graduated from high school when she was only 16. Sandra then left home to attend Stanford University in California. She graduated from law school in 1952, ranking third in her class of more than 100 students. While there, she served as the editor of the *Stanford Law Review*. After graduation, Sandra Day married one of her classmates, John J. O'Connor III.

A Seat in the Senate

Sandra and John O'Connor lived in Frankfurt, Germany, for a few years. John was a lawyer for the U.S. Army. Sandra worked as a lawyer also, but in the civilian quartermaster corps, drafting business contracts.

When the O'Connors returned to the U.S., they settled in Phoenix, Arizona. They had three sons, Brian, Jay, and Scott. While the boys were growing up, Sandra Day O'Connor worked part-time in her own

---

TOPICAL TIDBIT

Race for the Cure

Sandra Day O'Connor is a survivor of breast cancer. She participates each year in the Race for the Cure—an annual running race that raises funds for research, education, and treatment of breast cancer. Runners and sponsors of the cause wear pink ribbons to show their support.

law firm. She was appointed to the Arizona Governor's Committee on Marriage and Family and worked her way up through the ranks of the Arizona legal system. In 1965, she became the assistant attorney general for the state of Arizona.

In 1969, O'Connor was appointed by Governor Jack Williams to fill a vacant spot in the Arizona

Sandra Day O'Connor addresses students at a college graduation.

Senate. The following year, O'Connor was elected to the Senate on her own merits. She served two terms in that post.

The U.S. Supreme Court

In 1979, O'Connor was appointed to the Arizona Court of Appeals. In 1981, she spoke out regarding her belief that a state court's ruling on a case should be upheld—that is, the ruling should not be overturned by a federal court. O'Connor believed that state judges and federal judges should be equal in stature.

O'Connor's stance on the equality of judges gained her national recognition as a fair and impartial judge. In 1981, President Ronald Reagan nominated O'Connor to the U.S. Supreme Court. Upon her appointment, she became the first woman to hold the title of Supreme Court Justice since the national court was founded more than 200 years earlier.

During her time on the court, Justice O'Connor ruled on hundreds of cases. Although generally conservative, she was regarded as a compromiser. By virtue of her politically independent thinking, her vote was considered the "swing" vote on many cases brought before the Supreme Court. By 2004, O'Connor was considered one of the most powerful women in the world.

In addition to serving on the court, she also used

Sandra Day O'Connor

her talents to write about her personal experiences—on the ranch and on the bench. Her books include *Lazy B: Growing Up on a Cattle Ranch in the American Southwest* (2002) and *The Majesty of the Law: Reflections of a Supreme Court Justice* (2003). *Chico*, a children's book published in 2005, tells the adventures of young Sandra and her favorite horse.

On January 31, 2006, Sandra Day O'Connor retired from her 24-year position of Supreme Court Justice. Her hard work and fairness led the way for other women to serve at high levels in the U.S. court system. One of these women was Ruth Bader Ginsburg, who joined O'Connor on the bench in 1993.

LIFE EVENTS

1930
Sandra Day is born in El Paso, Texas.

1965
O'Connor becomes the assistant attorney general for the state of Arizona.

1970
O'Connor is elected to the U.S. Senate.

1981
President Ronald Reagan nominates O'Connor as a Supreme Court justice.

2004
Forbes Magazine lists O'Connor among the Top 10 Most Powerful Women in the World.

2006
O'Connor retires from the U.S. Supreme Court.

Georgia O'Keeffe
Painter
(born 1887 • died 1986)

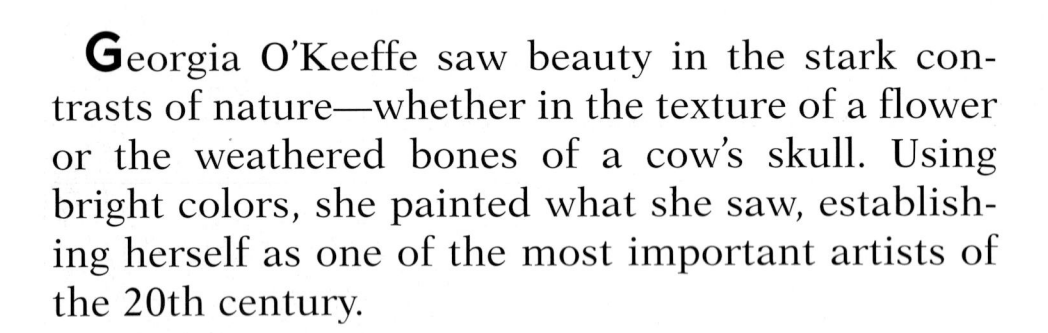

Georgia O'Keeffe saw beauty in the stark contrasts of nature—whether in the texture of a flower or the weathered bones of a cow's skull. Using bright colors, she painted what she saw, establishing herself as one of the most important artists of the 20th century.

Becoming a Painter

Georgia O'Keeffe was born on November 15, 1887, on a wheat farm near Sun Prairie, Wisconsin. She came from a big family—she had six brothers and sisters. Georgia dreamed of becoming an artist, so after graduating from high school, she left her family and moved to Illinois to attend the Art Institute of Chicago. In 1907, she headed to New York City. It was there that her dream came true. While attending the Art Students League, she received a prize for her still-life painting of a rabbit in a copper pot.

To earn a living, Georgia O'Keeffe took up teaching.

Georgia O'Keeffe

Georgia O'Keeffe stands with some of her work on display at the Whitney Museum of American Art in New York, in 1970.

In 1909, she accepted a teaching position in Texas. Later, she taught at Columbia Teachers College in South Carolina. In 1915, O'Keeffe accepted another teaching assignment—this time, she was to head the art department of West Texas State Normal College.

While in Texas, O'Keeffe painted colorful flowers and striking landscapes. She captured desert scenes of the Southwest like no one had ever before. She sent some of her work to a friend in New York, who showed them to Alfred Stieglitz, a noted photographer and owner of the 291 Gallery. Stieglitz exhibited O'Keeffe's paintings without her knowing about it. The fresh style of the paintings excited the New York art world, and a startled O'Keeffe hurried to New York to see what was going on. She and Stieglitz met and fell in love. She moved to New York in 1918, and the two were married in 1924.

> "Before I put a brush to canvas I question, 'Is this mine? Is it all intrinsically of myself?'"
> —Georgia O'Keeffe

Painting New Mexico

Each year, O'Keeffe's paintings were displayed in Stieglitz's gallery. While living in New York, she painted giant flowers and views of the city. By 1928, she was famous for these paintings. When she received $25,000 for her painting of a calla lily, she proved to the rest of the world that a female artist could, in fact, earn a living by doing what she loves.

The following year, O'Keeffe traveled back to the Southwest—this time, to New Mexico. The wide, open spaces of New Mexico enchanted her. She could see for miles in the clear, dry air of the desert. Unfortunately, her life with Stieglitz was in New York City. So she bought a car—a Model A Ford, one of the first cars ever made. Each summer she tossed her canvases and paints in the back seat, and traveled to New Mexico.

O'Keeffe loved the New Mexico landscape—red, pink, yellow, and orange rock formations set against the blue sky. She would take long walks, noticing the bleached bones of long-dead cattle and other animals. She would paint these images and ship them back to New York and to a waiting world.

O'Keeffe Goes Home

Steiglitz died in 1946, and O'Keeffe moved to New Mexico. She bought a house near her favorite spot—Ghost Ranch. She painted the landscape that she loved, and other images from her life in New

TOPICAL TIDBIT

Dinosaurs Discovered at Ghost Ranch

In 1947, dinosaur bones were found in Ghost Ranch, New Mexico. The bones date back to the Triassic Period (about 220 million years ago). Scientists believe that the bones belong to the *Coelophysis* (*SEEL-uh-FYE-sis*) species of dinosaurs. *Coelophysis* averaged about nine feet long, with a long neck and a pointed head.

Mexico—mission churches, adobe houses, and cactus.

O'Keeffe's eyesight began to fail when she was 71. So she turned her talents to sculpting and pottery. O'Keeffe died in Santa Fe, New Mexico, on March 6, 1986. She was 98.

A Place in History

Today, Georgia O'Keeffe's paintings are exhibited in galleries and museums all over the world. A mural, titled "Sky Above Clouds IV," hangs in the Art Institute of Chicago, where she once attended school. In 1997, the Georgia O'Keeffe Museum in Santa Fe, New Mexico, opened to the public—a tribute to her work as one of the great American Modern artists.

LIFE EVENTS

1887
Georgia O'Keeffe is born near Sun Prairie, Wisconsin.

1907
O'Keeffe wins a prize for a still life.

1908
Alfred Steiglitz mounts an exhibition of European artists. It is many Americans' first exposure to Picasso, Matisse, and Cezanne.

1915
Steiglitz exhibits one of O'Keeffe's paintings.

1924
O'Keeffe and Steiglitz marry.

1946
Steiglitz dies and O'Keeffe moves to New Mexico.

1986
Georgia O'Keeffe dies at the age of 98.

Rosa Parks
Civil-rights Activist
(born 1913 • died 2005)

Rosa Parks made history in 1955, when she refused to give up her seat on the bus to a white man. Her actions sparked a bus boycott in Alabama, which influenced the course of history in the United States. By fighting a law that she thought was unfair, Rosa encouraged others to stand up for their beliefs.

Rosa Faces Prejudice

Rosa Louise McCauley was born on February 14, 1913, in Tuskegee, Alabama. She was the daughter of a teacher and a carpenter, and the granddaughter of former slaves. Rosa attended a progressive school for girls. Her teachers encouraged her to work hard and build self-confidence. Later, she attended Alabama State University. She then moved to Montgomery, Alabama, with her new husband, Raymond Parks.

Living in the South was difficult for many African Americans in those days. Alabama was segregated, which meant that black people were allowed only in certain areas. In the 1950s, African Americans were often called "coloreds." White people told blacks where they could sit, drink, eat, or swim. Laws were passed about the beaches African Americans could use, the schools they could attend, the water fountains they could use, and where they could sit in restaurants, buses, theaters, and trains.

White people always had better seats, schools, beaches, and the like. If a black person was found in a whites-only section, he or she could be arrested, jailed, and fined. Often, a black person was beaten for being in the wrong place. That was never the case if a white person wandered into a coloreds-only section.

A lot of tension existed between whites and blacks.

Rosa Parks

As an African American, Rosa Parks faced discrimination every day. She believed that segregation was unfair and that all people should be treated as equals. Parks joined the National Association for the Advancement of Colored People (NAACP), an organization that sought to end racism, segregation, and discrimination.

Standing Up by Sitting Down

Parks worked as a housekeeper and seamstress in Montgomery. She rode the bus to work. Because she was black, she had to sit in the coloreds-only section at the back of the bus. About 70 percent of Montgomery bus riders were black. They had to enter the bus in the front, pay their fare, exit the bus, then re-enter in the back because they were not allowed to walk through the white section.

On December 1, 1955, Parks got on the bus to head home after a long day of work. As the bus picked up additional passengers, more whites entered the bus. There were not enough seats for them. So, the bus driver told Parks and other blacks to give up their seats. Parks thought this was unfair, so she said no. By doing this, Parks was breaking the law. As a result, the bus driver had her arrested.

> "My only concern was to get home after a hard day's work."
> —Rosa Parks

Parks pleaded her case in court, but was found guilty. Montgomery's black citizens were outraged and organized a boycott of the town's bus system. The large black community no longer rode the bus—they walked or arranged car pools. This hurt the local economy and sent a message to racist lawmakers.

Civil Rights

The African American community was inspired by Parks's actions and came together. One of the boycott leaders was a young black minister named Dr. Martin Luther King Jr.

Both Parks and King were threatened with violence for leading the boycott. Someone tried to blow up King's home. The boycott lasted more than a year, ending when the U.S. Supreme Court ruled that Montgomery's bus segregation laws were unconstitutional.

TOPICAL TIDBIT

King of the Civil-rights Movement

The Montgomery bus boycott thrust Dr. Martin Luther King Jr. into the role of civil-rights leader. When blacks were not allowed to register to vote in Selma, Alabama, he led marches in protest. He urged blacks to fight prejudice without violence. Despite his dedication to nonviolent protest, Dr. King was murdered in 1968.

Rosa Parks

Rosa Parks arrives at court on February 24, 1956, more than two months after sparking the Montgomery bus boycott.

The Montgomery bus boycott became one of the key steps toward racial equality in the United States. Many people refer to it as the start of the civil-rights movement, a period of civil unrest and struggle for equal rights for African Americans.

Taking Pride

Rosa and her husband, Raymond, moved to Detroit, Michigan, in 1957, after receiving death threats in Alabama. She worked for U.S. Congressman John Conyers Jr. for many years.

Wanting to inspire African American teens to build their self-esteem and take pride in their heritage, she started the Rosa and Raymond Parks Institute for Self-Development in 1987. She received the Presidential Medal of Freedom in 1996 and the

Congressional Gold Medal of Honor in 1999 for her civil-rights work. A year later, *Time* magazine named Rosa Parks one of the 100 most influential people of the 20th century.

On October 24, 2005, Rosa Parks died of natural causes in Detroit. She was 92. Her death was mourned by people throughout the world. Before the funeral, Parks's body was sent to Montgomery, Alabama, for a public viewing. Then she was honored as the first woman to "lie in state" at the Lincoln Memorial in Washington, D.C. This allowed thousands of people to view her body and pay their respects. She was returned to Detroit, where more than 4,000 people attended her funeral, including politicians and religious leaders. Shortly after her death, a government facility in Detroit was renamed the Rosa Parks Federal Building.

LIFE EVENTS

1913
Rosa Louise McCauley is born in Tuskegee, Alabama.

1955
Rosa Parks refuses to give up her seat to a white man. The Montgomery bus boycott begins.

1956
The bus boycott ends.

1957
The Southern Christian Leadership Conference creates the annual Rosa Parks Freedom Award.

1999
Parks receives the Congressional Gold Medal of Honor.

2002
The Rosa Parks Story airs on CBS.

2005
Parks dies on October 24th.

Jeannette Rankin
First Woman Elected to Congress
(born 1880 • died 1973)

In an era when few women in the United States were allowed to vote, Jeannette Rankin ran for the U.S. House of Representatives and won. During her career, she worked to get the right to vote for all American women, and she campaigned to improve working conditions. She was strongly opposed to war and never backed down from her beliefs, despite intense pressure to do so.

Votes for Women

Born on June 11, 1880, in Montana, Jeannette Rankin was the daughter of a rancher and a schoolteacher. She was the oldest of seven children. Unlike most young women at that time who married early and had children, Jeannette attended college. She graduated from the University of Montana in 1902.

Jeannette Rankin tried various jobs after graduation, including teaching and sewing. In 1908, she studied to become a social worker at the New York School of Philanthropy, then went to work in Seattle, Washington. Rankin, however, soon turned her attention to campaigning for women's suffrage (the right to vote).

During that time, women in the U.S. did not have the right to vote in national elections. Many women, including Rankin, thought that this was unfair. Rankin worked tirelessly in the state of Montana to get women the right to vote. In 1914, Rankin had her first victory: Montana gave women the right to vote statewide. Rankin turned her efforts to convincing the rest of the country to do the same.

First Woman Elected to Congress

Rankin decided to run for Congress, seeking a Republican seat in the House of Representatives. In 1916, she won, becoming the first woman elected to Congress. Actually, she was one of the first women elected to office anywhere in the world.

Her victory was short-lived, however. War had been raging in Europe since 1914, but the United States had kept out of the conflict. Many Americans supported "isolationism," meaning that they thought the U.S. should stay out of Europe's problems. As the war continued, however, President Woodrow Wilson asked Congress to allow the U.S. to enter the war.

Fifty-one representatives, including Rankin, voted against going to war. Rankin was a pacifist, someone who believes strongly in resolving conflict through peaceful means. Despite the efforts of Rankin and other pacifists, U.S. troops entered World War I in 1917. Although others had voted against war, Rankin became the center of attention because she was the only woman. Many people thought that she was being soft because she was female. They wanted her to resign from Congress.

Rankin was tough. She ran for re-election in 1918, but lost. She continued to work for women's suffrage and other causes. Her perseverance paid off. In 1920, the 19th Amendment to the U.S. Constitution was approved by the states, granting women the right to vote nationally.

Opposing Another War

Rankin worked with pacifist groups for several decades. She ran for Congress again in 1940, and won. This time, Europe was engaged in World War II. For a time, Americans did not want to get involved in the conflict, which had begun in 1939. When the Japanese bombed a U.S. naval base in Pearl Harbor, Hawaii, on December 7, 1941, however, the antiwar feeling changed for many Americans.

> "You can no more win a war than you can win an earthquake."
> —Jeannette Rankin

President Franklin D. Roosevelt asked Congress to declare war on Japan. When it came time to vote, Rankin stuck by her convictions and voted no. She was the only member of Congress to do so. Her stand was very unpopular and she was harshly criticized. She did not seek re-election.

TOPICAL TIDBIT

Rankin's Pacifism

In voting against war, Jeannette Rankin said, "I want to stand by my country, but I cannot vote for war." She refused to send young men to fight when she, herself, could not do so. Once the war began, however, she supported the troops by selling Liberty Bonds, which raised money for the war effort.

Pacifist to the End

Rankin continued to work for peace for the rest of her life. In 1968, at age 87, she led a group of women, known as the Jeannette Rankin Brigade, in a march on Washington, D.C. The group called for an end to U.S. involvement in the Vietnam War.

Jeannette Rankin died in Carmel, California, on May 18, 1973. Although she was criticized for opposing World Wars I and II, today she is greatly respected for standing up for her beliefs. Rankin braved criticism as the sole woman in Congress and never wavered in her convictions. In 1993, she was inducted into the National Women's Hall of Fame. A bronze statue of her now stands in the Capitol building—the official home of the U.S. Congress—in Washington, D.C.

LIFE EVENTS

1880
Jeannette Rankin is born near Missoula, Montana.

1909
Rankin becomes a social worker.

1914
Rankin begins working for the National American Woman Suffrage Association. World War I breaks out in Europe.

1916
Rankin is elected to the U.S. House of Representatives. Her antiwar position loses her that seat two years later.

1940
Rankin is re-elected to the House of Representatives.

1968
Rankin leads an anti-war march in Washington, D.C. She dies in 1973.

Janet Reno
Attorney General of the U.S.
(born 1938)

In 1993, Janet Reno became the first woman to hold the office of Attorney General of the United States. Very outspoken against violent crimes, illegal drug sales, child abuse, and murder, Reno drafted and implemented laws to protect the citizens of the United States.

Alligators and Peacocks

Janet Reno was born on July 21, 1938, in Miami, Florida. Her parents, Henry and Jane, were both newspaper reporters. When Janet was eight, the Reno family moved to an area near the Everglades—a swampy, wilderness area in southern Florida, filled with birds, insects, snakes, and alligators.

Janet's mother was a local legend. She recited poetry, wrestled alligators, and kept snakes in the house as pets. The four Reno children helped their mother raise peacocks, all named Horace. The children were encouraged to play outdoors. Janet grew up riding horses, camping, sailing, swimming, and scuba diving. She also enjoyed listening to all types of music.

Janet moved to Ithaca, New York, to attend Cornell University and study chemistry. She later attended Harvard Law School, from which she received a law degree in 1963.

Rising to the Top

After law school, Janet Reno returned to Miami, but had a difficult time finding a job. At that time, few law firms were willing to hire women. But that did not stop Reno. She kept trying and finally was able to practice law with the firm of Brigham and Brigham. By 1971, Reno had become staff director of the Judiciary Committee of the Florida House of Representatives.

In 1978, Reno was elected to the post of state attorney for Dade County. During the first year in her new position, she was responsible for more than 900 employees and oversaw more than 100,000 legal cases.

Reno was elected as state attorney five times. During those 15 years, Reno helped reform the juvenile-justice system in Florida. She set up crime-prevention programs that helped keep young people away from drugs, gangs, and crime. She took action against fathers who did not pay child support. She also set up the drug court, which found new ways to punish nonviolent drug offenders and get them off drugs.

Janet Reno, U.S. Attorney General

Reno's hard work paid off. On March 12, 1993, she was sworn in as U.S. Attorney General under President Bill Clinton. As the first woman to hold this position, she promised to uphold the U.S. Constitution and to lead the U.S. Department of Justice, which is the legal administration for the entire country.

Janet Reno

One of the main duties of the U.S. attorney general is to protect the rights of citizens and individuals within the United States. Sometimes, Reno used force to defend these rights. At various times, she called in the National Guard, the Drug Enforcement Administration (DEA), and the Federal Bureau of Investigation (FBI) to carry out orders to protect citizens.

Sometimes, Reno had to make difficult decisions. In 1993, Reno ordered the FBI to investigate the Branch Davidian religious cult in Waco, Texas. A *cult* is a group of people who are devoted to a person or an idea. Cult members are often extreme in their beliefs. The Davidians were reported to have dangerous weapons. There were also reports that citizens, including children, were being held against their will. After nearly two months of negotiations with cult leaders, Reno ordered the FBI to seize the area. There were gunshots, and a huge fire broke out. In

> "In 1960, when I graduated from college, people told me a woman couldn't go to law school. And when I graduated from law school, people told me, "Law firms won't hire you." Thirty years later, no one has ever told me I couldn't be attorney general."
> —Janet Reno

the end, 103 people, including FBI agents, cult members, and children were killed. Reno expressed deep regret that the situation had not ended peacefully.

In 2000, Reno made another tough decision. Elian Gonzales was a young Cuban refugee who had illegally entered the U.S. Elian's relatives wanted him to stay with them in Florida, but his father wanted him returned to Cuba. After weeks of negotiating with the families, Reno ordered the National Guard to take the boy from his relatives and return him to his father. Many people were upset by the use of force, but Reno believed that she had done the right thing.

Proud of Her Work

Janet Reno served as U.S. Attorney General from 1993 until 2001. Throughout her term, Reno pro-

TOPICAL TIDBIT

Song of America

In 2005, Janet Reno attended the 47th Annual Grammy Awards, hoping to attract popular musicians for her latest project. Called *Song of America*, the 50-track recording will chronicle the history of the U.S., beginning in 1620 with the arrival of the Pilgrims. Reno believes that young people are greatly influenced by music, yet many don't feel a need to learn about their country's history. What better way to find out than by listening to the music of the time.

Janet Reno

tected the rights of U.S. citizens, especially children. Even after her term ended, Reno continued to offer her talents and experience to protect U.S. citizens. In 2004, she met with government leaders to offer advice on to how to deal with terrorist attacks on U.S. soil.

Reno has dedicated her life to protecting Americans and defending their rights. In 2002, she ran for governor in her home state of Florida, but lost in the Democratic primary. Although she leads a quieter life now, her work continues to inspire young men and women seeking careers in the legal profession.

LIFE EVENTS

1938
Janet Reno is born in Miami, Florida.

1960
Reno enrolls at Harvard Law School, one of only 16 women in a class of more than 500 students.

1971
Reno is named staff director of the Judiciary Committee in the Florida House of Representatives.

1978
Reno is named Florida state attorney.

1993-2001
Reno serves as U.S. attorney general—the first woman to hold the job.

2004
Reno testifies before the National Commission on Terrorist Attacks Upon the United States.

Sally Ride
First American Woman in Space
(born 1951)

Sally Ride soared to new heights in 1983 aboard the space shuttle *Challenger* as the first American woman in space. Through hard work, courage, and determination, this modern-day explorer broke barriers on her way to the top of the world.

Tennis or Physics?

Sally Kristen Ride was born in Encino, California, on May 26, 1951. As a young girl, Sally trained as an athlete, hoping to make professional tennis her career. Although she was good with a racket, she decided to explore other options. She enrolled at Stanford University to study literature and science. After receiving degrees in English and physics in 1973, she continued her studies. While working toward her doctorate degree in astrophysics, Ride accepted a job as a teaching assistant in laser physics at Stanford.

Sally Ride

Sally Ride and her fellow astronauts prepare to board the space shuttle *Challenger* at the Kennedy Space Center on June 18, 1983.

In 1977, the National Aeronautics and Space Administration (NASA) put out a call for scientists to join the space program. NASA was looking for technicians to conduct experiments in space, using advanced machinery. Ride fit the bill. She was just finishing her studies in astrophysics and wanted to become one of NASA's first female astronauts.

The *Challenger*

NASA received 8,000 applications from scientists for the space-shuttle missions; only 35 spots were available. Ride was one of six women selected for the program in 1978. First, she had to undergo training, including learning to fly high-speed planes. Once she had received her pilot's license and completed her astronaut training, she was given the title of mission specialist. Ride's duties included preparing the Space Transportation System (STS), commonly called the space shuttle, for flights into space.

The space shuttle was a new type of spacecraft at the time. Designed by NASA in 1981, the space shuttle was a reusable vehicle that carried people, scientific instruments, and satellites to space stations or other space vehicles orbiting Earth. Once the shuttle and its crew completed the mission, they returned to Earth. The shuttle was then refitted for the next flight. The shuttle that Sally Ride served aboard was called *Challenger*.

The *Challenger's* fourth flight into space was scheduled for June 18, 1983. The crew's mission was to set

---

TOPICAL TIDBIT

Valentina Tereshkova

In 1963, Soviet cosmonaut Valentina Tereshkova became the first woman in space. Her flight lasted three days, during which she completed 48 orbits around Earth. Upon touchdown, Tereshkova was given a hero's welcome. She was awarded the Soviet Union's highest honor—the Order of Lenin—as the first woman in space.

up several satellites in orbit around Earth, then return six days later. Ride was selected as the crew's flight engineer. Reporters and camera crews flocked to the launch pad, waiting for the *Challenger* to take off. All of America watched and listened as the announcer called off the countdown: "Ten, nine, eight, seven, six, five, four, three, two, one—Lift off!" Sally Ride became the first American woman in space.

> "You spend a year training just which dials to look at and when the time comes, all you want to do is look out the window. It's so beautiful."
>
> —Sally Ride, on traveling in space

Space and Beyond

In October 1984, Sally returned to space on the *Challenger's* 13th flight. The mission was to take pictures of Earth using specially designed cameras. The mission was a success, capturing never-before-seen images of Earth. Then, in 1986, Ride accepted new responsibilities for NASA in creating its Office of Exploration, charting out long-range plans for the space program.

Ride resigned from NASA in 1987, becoming a physics professor at the University of California, San Diego. From 1989 to 1996, she served as the director of the California Space Institute at the school.

Ride continues to make important contributions to

the field of science education. She has written several books for children, including *To Space and Back*, recollections from her time aboard the space shuttle. Other books include *Third Planet: Exploring the Earth from Space*, published in 1994, and *Exploring Our Solar System*, published in 2003.

In 2001, Ride took on a new challenge—starting her own business. Called Sally Ride Space, the company offers educational programs and materials geared to girls and women who wish to pursue careers in the fields of math, physics, and space exploration. Sally Ride flew into history as the first American woman in space. She explored the regions of space known only to a handful of people. Her courage in facing unknown challenges makes her a hero to women and girls everywhere.

LIFE EVENTS

1951
Sally Kristen Ride is born in Encino, CA.

1983
Ride becomes the first American woman in space.

1986
Ride creates NASA's Office of Exploration.

1987
Ride resigns from NASA.

1989
Ride becomes director of the California Space Institute.

2001
Ride founds Sally Ride Science, a company that offers programs to girls interested in science and mathematics.

2003
Ride is inducted into the Astronaut Hall of Fame.

Eleanor Roosevelt
Social Reformer and First Lady
(born 1884 • died 1962)

Eleanor Roosevelt was an important social activist and reformer, as well as First Lady. She was devoted to many social causes, including ending poverty and addressing race and women's issues. In many ways, she was ahead of her time in the issues she tackled, leaving an example for future generations to follow.

Overcoming Shyness

Anna Eleanor Roosevelt was born on October 11, 1884, in New York City. She was the niece of Theodore Roosevelt, who was president of the United States from 1901 to 1909. During Eleanor's childhood, both of her parents died and she was sent to live with her grandmother. Unlike her beautiful mother, Eleanor was a plain-looking girl. She was very shy and lacked self-confidence.

At 15, she was sent to a girls' school in England. There, Eleanor slowly overcame her shyness and gained confidence. The school's principal thought that Eleanor had strong leadership qualities.

Three years later, Eleanor returned to New York. Interested in social issues, she taught exercise and dance classes to people living in the city's poor neighborhoods. In 1903, she became engaged to

Franklin D. Roosevelt (known as FDR), a distant cousin. They married on March 17, 1905.

Life with FDR

FDR devoted his career to public service. During the first 11 years of marriage, FDR and Eleanor had five children. They also got involved in politics as Democrats. In 1910, FDR became a senator from New York, and Eleanor assisted her husband with his political duties.

> "I could not, at any age, be content to take my place by the fireside and simply look on. Life was meant to be lived, and curiosity must be kept alive. One must never, for whatever reason, turn his back on life."
>
> —Eleanor Roosevelt

In 1918, during World War I, Eleanor worked with the American Red Cross and volunteered in Navy hospitals.

In 1921, FDR contracted polio, a crippling disease that affected his legs, making it difficult to walk. Encouraged by Eleanor, FDR continued in politics despite his disability. She often traveled around the country to see what was happening in different communities across the states. Then she reported her findings to FDR. In 1928, he was elected governor of New York.

Eleanor pursued her own interests too. She and some of her women friends—all of whom were activists—built a rustic cottage north of New York City. In 1926, they co-founded Val-kill Industries, a furniture factory there. It was designed to give jobs to local youths and to keep the local economy strong.

Becoming the First Lady

In 1933, FDR became the 32nd president of the United States. At that time, many politicians' wives stayed in the background. Not Eleanor. She took up women's and civil-rights causes. She openly disagreed with FDR when she believed that she should speak out. Unlike other politicians, FDR truly respected his wife and her ideals. Even as president, he frequently asked Eleanor's advice.

FDR was reelected three times. During FDR's 12 years in office, he and Eleanor saw the nation through

TOPICAL TIDBIT

The Four-term President

Franklin Delano Roosevelt was the only U.S. president to be elected four times. In 1951, the 22nd Amendment to the Constitution was ratified. It states that no person can be elected to the presidency more than two times.

the Great Depression and World War II. During the Depression, FDR established work programs to keep people employed, and Eleanor made sure that women and minorities were included in those programs. During the war, the Roosevelts built morale for the American public and put women to work in jobs left by men who had been sent to the front lines.

Eleanor began holding press conferences at the White House. She was the first First Lady to do so. When she started inviting only female journalists to the press conferences, she forced many of the nation's top newspapers to hire female reporters for the first time.

A Continuing Influence

Eleanor Roosevelt continued to influence history. She wrote her own newspaper column, called "My Day," from 1935 until her death. She fought to end racial segregation laws, which created separate areas—such as beaches, parks, schools—for whites and blacks. At a meeting in Alabama in 1939, she caused a stir by sitting in the black section of seats instead of the whites-only section. With her help, segregation ended in the Army Nurse Corps in 1945.

When FDR died in 1945, Eleanor thought that her political career was over. However, the new president, Harry S. Truman, appointed her as U.S. delegate to the United Nations (UN). In 1947, she led the UN's Human Rights Commission in creating the Declaration of

Human Rights. In 1961, President John F. Kennedy appointed her as first chairperson of the President's Commission on the Status of Women.

Eleanor Roosevelt died on November 7, 1962, in New York City. She had always shown great sensitivity to others, and was respected and admired by people worldwide.

Many historians believe that Eleanor Roosevelt achieved more than any other First Lady. She furthered women's rights, human rights, and civil rights in the U.S. and abroad. She was inducted into the National Women's Hall of Fame, and named one of the most influential people of the 20th century by *Time* magazine. People can visit her cottage home, now called the Eleanor Roosevelt National Historic Site, in Hyde Park, New York.

LIFE EVENTS

1884
Anna Eleanor Roosevelt is born in New York City.

1905
Eleanor marries Franklin Delano Roosevelt (FDR).

1933
FDR begins his first term as president.

1945
President Truman appoints Eleanor Roosevelt as a delegate to the United Nations (UN).

1948
Eleanor Roosevelt is a major contributor to the UN's Universal Declaration of Human Rights.

1958
On My Own, Roosevelt's autobiography, is published. She dies in 1962.

Wilma Rudolph
Track-and-Field Star
(born 1940 • died 1994)

Wilma Rudolph was a sickly child, often confined to bed. Childhood diseases had left her weak and without the use of one of her legs. Yet she was determined to overcome her disability. Rudolph learned to walk without a leg brace—then went on to become one of the fastest runners in the world.

Overcoming Obstacles

When Wilma Glodean Rudolph was born on June 23, 1940, in St. Bethlehem, Tennessee, she was a premature baby. She weighed only four and a half pounds. While still a child, she survived scarlet fever, pneumonia, and polio. Polio, which is a disease of the spinal cord, left Wilma unable to use one of her legs.

Wilma came from a large family, and her brothers and sisters tried to help her by massaging her leg. She also took physical therapy to make her leg work better. Wilma used a leg brace to help her walk. As she grew older, she got stronger and, eventually, she

50 American Women

Wilma Rudolph runs the last leg of a relay race.

could walk without help. By the time she was 11, she had started to play basketball.

Wilma played on the basketball team in high school and became a star athlete. Despite her successes, she still faced an obstacle: racial discrimination. As an

Wilma Rudolph

African American growing up in the South, she was treated as an inferior person. The South was segregated, which means that blacks and whites had to use separate public facilities. For example, there were separate beaches, parks, schools, bathrooms, and water fountains. The facilities for whites were better than those for blacks.

Running for the Gold

In high school, Wilma Rudolph got involved in track, and proved that the color of her skin had nothing to do with her ability as an athlete. At 5 feet, 11 inches tall, Rudolph had long legs and could run fast. She was so fast, in fact, that she qualified for the Olympics in 1956 and represented the U.S. at the Games in Melbourne, Australia. Rudolph participated in the 4x100–meter

TOPICAL TIDBIT

Overcoming Polio

Other famous people have battled polio and gone on to achieve their dreams. President Franklin D. Roosevelt was a polio survivor. He saw the country through World War II and the worst economic depression in history. The Mexican painter Frida Kahlo was also a polio survivor. She used bright colors on canvas to express her pain and struggle.

relay, a competition in which four team members each run one part of the race. She and her team won a bronze medal (third place).

Beginning in 1957, Rudolph attended Tennessee State University and continued to run track. In 1960, she set a world record for the 200-meter race at 22.9 seconds. That same year, she returned to the Summer Olympics, this time in Rome, Italy. Several other women from Tennessee State joined her on the U.S. track team. Rudolph dazzled the crowds with her speed.

> "Never underestimate the power of dreams and the influence of the human spirit. We are all the same in this notion: The potential for greatness lives within each of us."
> —Wilma Rudolph

At the Olympics, Rudolph won three gold medals, becoming the first American woman to do so at one Olympic competition. She won both the 100- and 200-meter races. Her team also took home first place in the 4 x 100–meter relay.

After the Olympics, Rudolph continued to compete, and fans flocked to see her. Once, in Germany, a fan stole her shoes as a souvenir.

When Rudolph returned home to Tennessee, a parade was held in her honor. It was extra special for Rudolph because it was the first nonsegregated parade held in her hometown. In the years that followed, Rudolph married and had four children. She worked with groups, such as Operation Champion, that helped inner-city children. She also set up the Wilma Rudolph Foundation, which provides athletic coaching and educational support for underprivileged children.

Into the History Books

Wilma Rudolph died of brain cancer on November 12, 1994, in Brentwood, Tennessee. Her courageous spirit and amazing talent still inspire people around the world. She was inducted into the National Track and Field Hall of Fame, the U.S. Olympic Hall of Fame, and the National Women's Hall of Fame. Her autobiography, *Wilma*, was made into a TV movie. Today, she is remembered as one of the fastest women who ever lived.

LIFE EVENTS

1940
Wilma Glodean Rudolph is born in St. Bethlehem, Tennessee.

1956
Rudolph wins a team bronze medal at the Olympics.

1960
Rudolph sets a world record, and becomes the first female U.S. runner to win three gold medals at one Olympics.

1980
Rudolph is inducted into the International Sports Hall of Fame (and to two other Halls of Fame in 1974 and 1983).

1982
Rudolph founds the Wilma Rudolph Foundation.

1994
Rudolph dies.

Sacagawea
Interpreter and Explorer
(born about 1787 • died 1812 or 1884)

Sacagawea *(SAK-uh-juh-WEE-ah)*, a Shoshone Indian, helped lead explorers Lewis and Clark to the far west regions of the United States in the early 1800s. Hired as an interpreter and guide, Sacagawea joined the famous team on its journey in search of land and water routes to the Pacific Ocean.

Sacagawea Is Kidnapped

Sacagawea was born into the Shoshone tribe in Idaho around 1787. She was the daughter of a Shoshone chief. When she was 12 years old, she was kidnapped by warriors of the rival Hidatsa tribe and taken as a slave to their village along the Missouri River in North Dakota.

The Hidatsa sold Sacagawea as a bride to French-Canadian fur trapper Toussaint Charbonneau. In February 1805 Sacagawea gave birth to a son. They named him Jean Baptiste Charbonneau.

Sacagawea Becomes an Explorer

About the time that Sacagawea was kidnapped, people living in the eastern U.S. were curious about the vast, unexplored area between the Missouri River and the Pacific Ocean. President Thomas Jefferson sent a team of explorers, led by Meriwether Lewis and William Clark, to scout the area. Lewis's task was to study the plants and wildlife, while Clark was to make maps of the region. The expedition was called the Corps of Discovery.

On May 21, 1804, the explorers set out from St. Louis, Missouri. They set up camp for the winter in North Dakota, where they met Charbonneau and Sacagawea. The group knew that they would meet many native people along the way who did not speak English. Since Lewis and Clark spoke only English and one of the group's officers spoke French, they

TOPICAL TIDBIT

Bird Woman or Boat Launcher?

Sacagawea's name has been spelled with a *g* and with a *j*. *Sacagawea* means "bird woman" in Hidatsa. *Sacajawea* with a *j*, however, means "boat launcher" in Shoshone. This pronunciation, *sak-uh-juh-WEE-ah*, is the most common. In his journals, however, William Clark was very careful to point out that the name of his interpreter was pronounced *sah-kah-gah-WEE-ah*.

Sacagawea guides Lewis and Clark.

hired Sacagawea and her husband as interpreters. Sacagawea spoke Shoshone and Hidatsa; Charbonneau spoke Hidatsa and French.

The group left North Dakota in April 1805. Using horses and canoes, they made their way through the wilderness of Idaho, Montana, Oregon, and

◇ Sacagawea ◇

Washington. As they roamed through the forests, Sacagawea collected nuts and berries for food, while carrying her infant son in a cradleboard (knapsack) on her back.

Once the expedition reached the Bitterroot Mountains of Idaho, they needed 30 horses to transport their supplies. They found a Shoshone tribe living nearby, so they asked Sacagawea to trade some goods for the horses. When she approached the tribal chief, she discovered that it was her brother Cameahwait *(kah-MAY-uh-wah-it)*. She had not seen him since she was kidnapped.

> "Sacagawea was sent for; she came into the tent, sat down, and was beginning to interpret, when in the person of Cameahwait she recognised her brother: She instantly jumped up, and ran and embraced him."
> —from the Lewis & Clark journals

After a tearful but joyous reunion, Sacagawea traded for the horses. She spoke with her brother in her native tongue of Shoshone and translated his response into Hidatsa. Charbonneau then translated the words from Hidatsa into French. The expedition's French-speaking officer translated the words into English so that Lewis and Clark and the other members of the group could follow the conversation.

The Explorers Return

The expedition reached the Columbia River in November 1805. The men built a shelter, which they named Fort Clatsop, to protect the team from the harsh winter weather. They stayed at the fort until spring, getting by with barely enough to eat.

When the snow melted, the group headed back to St. Louis. Sacagawea led the expedition through her homeland, following old Indian trails. When they reached the banks of the Missouri River in North Dakota, after traveling nearly 4,000 miles, Sacagawea and Charbonneau stayed; the team went on.

In 1812, Sacagawea had another baby, named Lisette. On December 20, later that year, Sacagawea

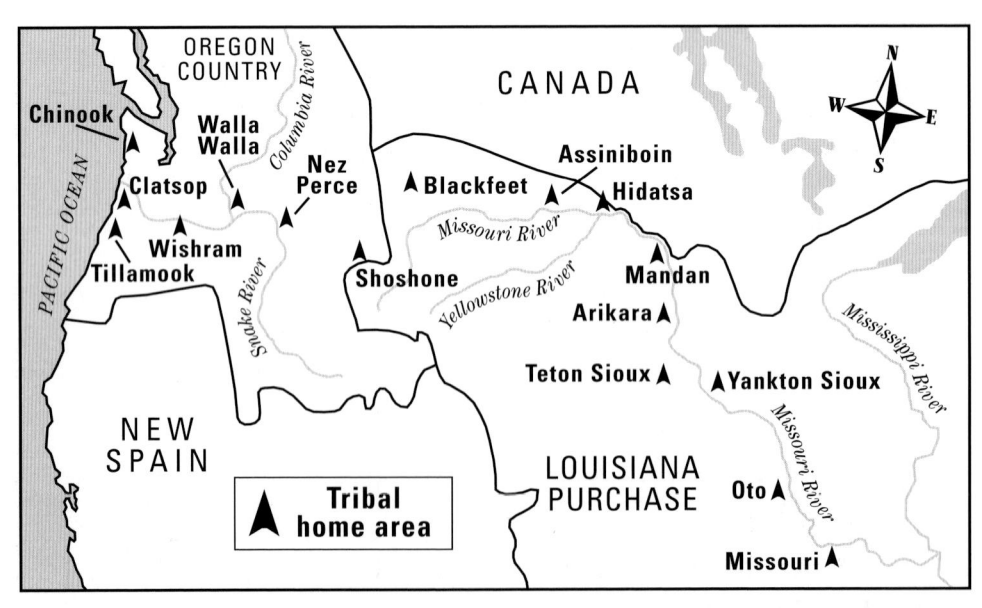

The Corps of Discovery encountered many different Native American tribes on its journey.

died. William Clark adopted both children. According to the Shoshone, however, Sacagawea did not die in 1812, but remarried and took the name Porivo. Porivo lived on the Wind River Reservation, and knew many details of Lewis and Clark's journey. She died on April 9, 1884.

A True American Hero

With Sacagawea's help, William Clark was able to map an uncharted wilderness, establishing trails and landmarks for later pioneers. The Corps of Discovery gathered information about the geography, people, and wildlife of the western U.S. Many memorials have been dedicated to Sacagawea. Clark also named a river after his skillful guide. Sacagawea is traditionally known as the first woman to travel overland and see the "great waters" of the Pacific Ocean.

LIFE EVENTS

About 1787
Sacagawea is born.

About 1800
Sacagawea is kidnapped, sold to Mandan Indians, then to a French-Canadian fur trapper.

1804
Meriwether Lewis and William Clark start from St. Louis, Missouri, on their journey north and west.

1805
Sacagawea meets Lewis and Clark in what is now North Dakota. She, her husband, and baby son accompany the expedition. The team returns in 1806.

2000
The U.S. Mint issues new one-dollar coins. Sacagawea appears on the face of the coin.

Elizabeth Cady Stanton
Women's Rights Leader
(born 1815 • died 1902)

During the 1800s, Elizabeth Cady Stanton and Susan B. Anthony led the crusade for women's rights in the U.S. United in the cause of women's suffrage—the right to vote—they worked together for more than 50 years to bring about change in the United States. A devoted wife and mother of seven children, Stanton wrote speeches for Anthony to present across the country, while she stayed at home to raise her children.

"I Wish You Were a Boy!"
On November 12, 1815, Elizabeth Cady was born in Johnstown, New York. She was one of six children, mostly girls. When Elizabeth's brother died, her father was very upset. He said to her, "Oh my daughter, I wish you were a boy!" Elizabeth tried to be like a son to her father. She studied very hard in

Elizabeth Cady Stanton

Elizabeth Cady Stanton *(right)* poses with Susan B. Anthony *(left)*.

school, learning math, philosophy, Greek, and Latin. She loved to go horseback riding and debate political issues—something that few girls ever did.

Elizabeth's father was a congressman and New York Supreme Court judge. Elizabeth spent hours studying law in her father's office. It was there that she learned about the unfair advantages that men had over women. She decided that she would work to make women equal to men in the eyes of the law.

"We Hold These Truths . . ."

In 1840 Elizabeth married Henry Stanton, a lawyer and abolitionist—someone who believed that slavery should be abolished (outlawed). They spent their honeymoon in London, England, so that Elizabeth could attend the World Anti-Slavery convention. Several women went to the convention, but were turned away because they were women. One of those women was Lucretia Mott. Elizabeth and Mott became good friends and, over the years, talked of women's rights issues.

On July 19-20, 1848, in Seneca Falls, New York, Stanton and Mott gathered together more than 100 women to discuss the issue of women's rights. The Seneca Falls Convention, as it is now called, was the beginning of the women's rights movement.

At the meeting, Stanton read the "Declaration of Sentiments"—a document based on the Declaration of Independence. The opening lines of the declaration read: "We hold these truths to be self-evident: that all men AND WOMEN are created equal." The

TOPICAL TIDBIT

Lucretia Mott

Lucretia Mott (1793-1880) believed that all people should be treated as equals. As one of the founders of the American Anti-Slavery Society, Mott devoted her energy to freeing African American slaves, including running a station on the Underground Railroad. Later, she worked with Elizabeth Cady Stanton to launch the women's rights movement.

declaration states that women should be treated equally and fairly by the laws governing the United States. It also states that women should be allowed to vote, just like any other citizen in the country.

The Crusade for Women's Suffrage

A few years later, Stanton met Susan B. Anthony. For the next 50 years, the two worked together, crusading for women's suffrage. In 1869, they formed the National Woman Suffrage Association. Stanton served as president of the group until 1890.

Stanton was an excellent writer and lecturer. She wrote many articles for newspapers and magazines, and also wrote several books, including *The History of Woman Suffrage*, with Susan B. Anthony and Matilda Joslyn Gage.

Stanton also drafted an amendment (change) to the U.S. Constitution, calling for the U.S. government to grant women the right to vote. Beginning in 1878, Anthony and other suffragists appeared before

> "The prejudice against color, of which we hear so much, is no stronger than that against sex. It is produced by the same cause, and manifested very much in the same way."
> —Elizabeth Cady Stanton

Congress each year to propose the amendment. When Stanton died, on October 26, 1902, the amendment still had not become law. Not until 1920 was the amendment, the 19th Amendment, finally added to the U.S. Constitution. Later that year, more than 8 million women voted for the first time in U.S. history.

Never to Be Forgotten

Elizabeth Cady Stanton devoted her life to women's rights issues. Although she was never honored during her lifetime as one of the founders of the women's rights movement, she will always be remembered as such. A statue of Stanton, Anthony, and Mott stands in the U.S. Capitol in Washington, D.C. Stanton also has been inducted into the National Women's Hall of Fame in Seneca Falls, New York.

LIFE EVENTS

1815
Elizabeth Cady is born in Johnstown, New York.

1848
Elizabeth Cady Stanton and Lucretia Mott organize the world's first women's rights convention.

1851
Stanton meets Susan B. Anthony.

1869
Stanton and Anthony found the National Woman Suffrage Association.

1878
Stanton drafts an amendment to the Constitution that would grant women the right to vote. She dies in 1902.

1920
The 19th Amendment, granting women the right to vote, is ratified.

Gloria Steinem
Journalist and Feminist
(born 1934)

"A woman without a man is like a fish without a bicycle," said Gloria Steinem, leader of the feminist movement. The point that Steinem was making with this statement is that women do not need to be dependent upon men for their survival. Women can make choices for themselves and should not be discriminated against because of their gender.

On the Road

Gloria Marie Steinem was born in Toledo, Ohio, on March 25, 1934, to Ruth and Leo Steinem. Gloria's father was an antiques dealer. Most of the year, the Steinem family traveled around the country in a trailer so that Leo could sell antiques. The family spent their summers in Michigan, where they owned a small resort. Gloria and her older sister, Susan, did not attend school like other children because the family moved from town to town. The girls were taught by their mother, who had been a teacher.

When Gloria was 10, her parents divorced. Susan went off to college, while Gloria lived with her mother in Toledo. Ruth Steinem was very sick—she suffered from depression—and Gloria was left to take care of her. Gloria went to public school in Toledo and became very independent. It was up to her to clean, shop for groceries, and run the house.

Gloria excelled at school. She spent her senior year of high school in Washington, D.C., with her sister, while her father took care of Ruth. Gloria thrived. She was then accepted to Smith College, where Susan had gone.

At Smith College, Gloria studied government and politics. She spent a year in Geneva, Switzerland, as an exchange student. She also wrote articles for the college newspaper. As Gloria became more politically active, she realized that her mother's illness was not always taken seriously because she was a woman. Gloria decided to change things for women throughout the world.

> "I'm optimistic [about the future]. But I also know nothing will happen automatically. Change depends on what you and I do every day."
> —Gloria Steinem

Becoming a Feminist

In 1956, Gloria Steinem received a scholarship to study in India. When Steinem returned to the U.S. two years later, she published a book about her experience called *A Thousand Indias*. Steinem hoped that this would help her land a career in journalism. However, many newspaper and magazine editors turned her down for jobs because she was a woman. They wanted a serious journalist, not a "pretty girl."

Steinem was furious. Why did these men think that a woman could not be a professional journalist?

Steinem eventually became an editorial assistant for *Help!* magazine. She met people in the business and began writing freelance articles. In 1963, on an assignment for *Esquire* magazine, she went undercover as a "bunny" at New York's Playboy Club. Playboy bunnies were cocktail waitresses who wore skimpy outfits and bunny ears. Steinem's article, "I Was a Playboy Bunny," talked about sexual harassment and discrimination against women at the club. Steinem thought that it would be her ticket to serious journalism. She was wrong. The editors looked past her writing talent and saw her only as a Playboy bunny.

TOPICAL TIDBIT

Ms. Magazine

In 1972, a magazine published by women hit the newsstands. *Ms.* magazine, founded by Gloria Steinem and Dorothy Pitman Hughes, was dedicated to addressing the concerns of women throughout the world. Article topics include past and present political trends in the women's movement, women's rights, women's health issues, and social issues that face young and older women today.

Crusading for Women's Rights

Through hard work and determination, Steinem finally achieved her goal. In 1968, she became an editor for *New York* magazine. The job gave her the opportunity to choose her own assignments. She wrote about the assassination of Dr. Martin Luther King Jr., labor-union strikes, and women's liberation. In December 1971, Steinem, along with Dorothy Pitman Hughes, founded *Ms.*, a magazine geared to women's political and social issues. Steinem was named Woman of the Year by *McCall's* magazine in 1972.

As an outspoken, intelligent activist, Steinem became a leader of the women's rights movement. She founded many women's groups, including the National Women's Political Caucus and the Coalition of Labor Union Women. These groups spoke out about women's issues, such as freedom of choice (legalized abortion), equal pay for equal work, and sex discrimination.

The Crusade Continues

Steinem served as editor of *Ms.* magazine for 16 years. In addition, she has written books on the world of publishing and women's rights, including *Revolution from Within*, published in 1992, and *Moving Beyond Words*, published in 1994. She has also appeared in several films and television documentaries, including *No Safe Place: Violence Against Women*, which aired in 1998, and *One Bright Shining Moment*, released in 2005.

Throughout her career, Steinem has received many awards. In 1993, she was inducted into the National Women's Hall of Fame. She is one of the most famous and outspoken feminists of the 20th and 21st centuries, and she remains a crusader for the rights of women.

LIFE EVENTS

1934
Gloria Marie Steinem is born in Toledo, Ohio.

1963
Steinem publishes a feminist article on working at the Playboy Club.

1971
Steinem co-founds the National Women's Political Caucus and *Ms.*, a feminist magazine.

1972
Steinem is named Woman of the Year by *McCall's* magazine.

1973
Steinem helps found the Coalition of Labor Union Women.

2005
Steinem receives the Missouri Honor Medal for Distinguished Service in Journalism.

Ida M. Tarbell
Investigative Reporter
(born 1857 • died 1944)

Ida M. Tarbell began a career in journalism in the late 19th century. She approached her work differently from most reporters of her day—she investigated her subjects thoroughly. Most journalists only touched the surface of a story, because getting it out first was more important than getting a full story. But Tarbell dug deep to uncover the truth. Tarbell's style of journalism became popular, and today she is recognized as one of America's first investigative reporters.

Early Influences

Ida Minerva Tarbell was born on November 5, 1857, in Erie County, Pennsylvania. Her father, Franklin, owned a small, independent oil company and her mother, Esther, was interested in furthering women's rights, such as the right to vote and the right to own property.

Ida was a curious child. She liked to explore, study,

Ida M. Tarbell poses with a statue of President Abraham Lincoln.

and read. Interested in her father's oil business, she learned about science and the natural world. She became aware of the problems that her father had in business. He worked independently, which meant that he was not part of a big business. As the oil industry boomed, big businesses began pushing out the independents, taking over their operations. Ida's father had a difficult time keeping his company going.

Despite the family's financial troubles, Ida went to college. In the 1870s, few teenage girls planned to attend college or start a career. They were expected to become good wives and stay at home and raise many children. Ida Tarbell had other plans. She entered Allegheny College, which had just started to allow female students. She graduated in 1880.

> "Nobody begins or ends anything. Each person is a link, weak or strong, in an endless chain."
>
> —Ida Tarbell, from her autobiography

Ida Becomes a Journalist

Ida Tarbell found work as a schoolteacher in Ohio, but left that position after two years. In 1883, she joined the staff of a small magazine. Eight years later, she did something that most women of her day would never dream of doing: She went to Paris, France, to live and study.

To support herself in Paris, Tarbell worked as a freelance writer. She returned to the U.S. in 1894 and began work as a reporter at *McClure's Magazine*.

The reporters at *McClure's* were among the first to take up investigative reporting. They wrote about social issues, and exposed corruption in government, politics, and big business. President Theodore Roosevelt called such reporters "muckrakers," because he believed that they would do anything—even rake through mud and muck—to dig up a story.

Tarbell's first assignments were biographies on such people as President Abraham Lincoln. She then began a long investigation into the Standard Oil Company, one of the big businesses that squeezed out smaller, independent oil companies, like her father's. Her series of articles was published as a book, *The History of the Standard Oil Company*, in 1904.

Tarbell's findings led to a government investigation of Standard Oil's illegal practices, and the case

---

TOPICAL TIDBIT

From Yellow to Muck

Before "muckraking" became a popular form of journalism in the U.S., many newspapers hired reporters who sensationalized stories. These reporters twisted and exaggerated the facts to make stories more appealing to readers. Such reporters wrote about sex scandals and violence, among other topics. This type of reporting was known as Yellow Journalism.

Ida M. Tarbell

was brought to trial. In 1911, the U.S. Supreme Court ruled that Standard Oil had an unfair monopoly—it controlled too much of the oil business in the U.S. The Court ordered that the company be split into smaller, separate businesses.

Changing Attitudes

Tarbell's work made her a popular journalist. In 1906, she and several other *McClure's* writers left their jobs to start their own publication, *American Magazine*. Tarbell continued to write on social issues for the magazine until 1915. She also wrote books, including *The Business of Being a Woman* (1912).

As Tarbell grew older, her ideas about women and careers changed. She suggested that women avoid working outside the home.

LIFE EVENTS

1857
Ida Minerva Tarbell is born in Erie County, Pennsylvania.

1894-1906
Tarbell works as a staff writer for *McLure's* Magazine.

1904
Tarbell publishes *The History of the Standard Oil Company*, a critique of J. D. Rockefeller's business practices.

1906-1915
Tarbell writes and edits for *American Magazine*, which she helped found.

1912
Tarbell publishes *The Business of Being a Woman*.

1939
Tarbell's autobiography, *All in the Day's Work*, is published.

1944
Tarbell dies.

Tarbell no longer supported many women's rights issues, including a woman's right to vote. Some people thought that Tarbell was turning her back on the very movement that had helped her succeed in a man's world. Her new attitudes hurt her popularity.

A Journalist to the End

Tarbell continued to write into her eighties, penning her autobiography *All in a Day's Work*. She died on January 6, 1944, in Bridgeport, Connecticut. Despite her later ideas about working women, Tarbell had a successful career as an investigative reporter. She was one of the first women to excel in journalism. She was inducted into the National Women's Hall of Fame in 2000.

Sojourner Truth
Crusader for African American Rights
(born about 1797 • died 1883)

Standing six feet tall, Sojourner Truth had a powerful presence. As a freed slave, she traveled throughout the North preaching religion, abolition (ending slavery), and women's rights. She was a strong speaker, even though she had never been taught to read or write. In an era of limited opportunities for women, especially black women, Sojourner Truth was an inspiring activist.

A Slave in the North

Sojourner Truth's story is different from those of many others born into slavery. She was born around 1797 in Ulster County, New York. At that time, slavery was allowed in parts of the North, as well as in the South. Her name was Isabella. Like many slaves, she had no last name. Isabella was one of 10 children, but most of her brothers and sisters had been sold and sent away to work for other families.

Unlike slaves in the South, most of whom worked on large plantations, Isabella tended to crops and housekeeping chores on a farm owned by a Dutch family. As a result, she spoke Dutch. People later remarked that she had an unusual voice because she spoke English with a Dutch accent. Isabella married a slave named Thomas and had five children. She was devastated when several of her children were sold to other slave holders.

The government of New York State ended the practice of slavery on July 4, 1827, and Isabella was set free. She began living with another family, the Van Wageners, and used their last name as her own.

Isabella went to court to try to free her young son, Peter, who was a slave in Alabama. She won her case and the two were joyfully reunited. Isabella and two of her children moved to New York City about 1829. Isabella worked as a housekeeper.

> "If the first woman God ever made was strong enough to turn the world upside down all alone, these women together ought to be able to turn it back, and get it right side up again! And now they is asking to do it, the men better let them."
> —Sojourner Truth, at the Women's Convention in Akron, Ohio, in 1851

A Religious Experience

Isabella was a deeply religious person and often preached on the streets of New York. Throughout her life, she said that she heard voices and had visions sent by God. In 1843, a voice told her to change her name to "Sojourner Truth," as she was to "walk in truth." Her name change signaled a new chapter in her life: She set out on the road to preach and sing about the gospel (God's word).

Sojourner Truth found a new home at the Northampton Association of Education and Industry in Florence, Massachusetts. It was a cooperative farm—a place where like-minded people lived, worked, and shared resources. Members of the community believed in equality, abolition, and other human rights. There, she met antislavery crusaders Frederick Douglass, William Lloyd Garrison, and Olive Gilbert. While at Northampton, Truth also took up the cause of women's equality.

Olive Gilbert helped Truth publish her first book. Since Truth could not read or write, she told her story to Gilbert, who wrote it down. The book was

TOPICAL TIDBIT

In the Shadows

Sojourner Truth had a limited income from her book sales, so she raised additional money by selling her photograph. Many speakers of the day did the same thing. In that era, photos were sometimes called "shadows." Truth's photo included the caption: "I Sell the Shadow to Support the Substance [herself]."

Sojourner Truth

published in 1850 as *The Narrative of Sojourner Truth: A Northern Slave*. She supported herself with money from her book sales.

Truth also began lecturing about abolition and women's rights. She was a dynamic speaker who moved the audience with her wit and wisdom. At a women's convention in Akron, Ohio, in 1851, Truth gave what became her most famous speech. One by one, she knocked down reasons men often gave for why women were inferior to men. With each argument, she repeated "And ain't I a woman?" to prove her point.

The Work Continues

The Northampton Association broke up in 1846, and Truth remained in Florence before moving to Battle Creek, Michigan, in 1857. She continued to travel to support her

---

LIFE EVENTS

1797
Sojourner Truth is born a slave named Isabelle in Ulster County, New York.

1827
Isabelle is freed when New York State law abolishes slavery.

1850
Truth publishes *The Narrative of Sojourner Truth.*

1851
Truth becomes active in the suffrage movement.

1863
The Emancipation Proclamation is signed, freeing slaves in Confederate states.

1883
Sojourner Truth dies in Michigan.

causes. She even met with President Abraham Lincoln. During the Civil War (1861-1865), Truth raised money and supplies for black troops.

After the war, Truth asked Congress to set aside public lands to create a "Negro state." She also worked with former slaves to help them adjust to life as free individuals. She died on November 26, 1883, in Michigan, possibly from diabetes.

Sojourner Truth used her life experience to help others understand the important struggles facing the U.S. before and after the Civil War. Her work has been recognized in many ways, including induction into the National Women's Hall of Fame. Residents of Florence, Massachusetts, are building a statue in her honor.

Harriet Tubman
Conductor on the Underground Railroad
(born about 1820 • died 1913)

Harriet Tubman risked her life to help slaves escape from the South before the Civil War (1861-1865). A former slave herself, Harriet faced jail, a return to slavery, or even death if she was caught. Regardless, she returned to the South again and again to lead others to freedom via the Underground Railroad. Tubman succeeded in helping many blacks find new, free lives.

Meager Beginnings

Harriet was born Araminta Greene around 1820 in Bucktown, Maryland. She later changed her name to Harriet, after her mother. Her parents, Harriet Greene and Benjamin Ross, were black slaves who were not allowed to marry. Laws in the South severely restricted what blacks could do. Slaves were treated like property, and white owners could sell them at will, as a farmer might sell a cow or horse. Slave owners split up many black families that way. Marriage was not allowed because owners did not want their slaves to become too attached to one another.

As a slave, young Harriet worked the fields, chopped wood, cleaned the master's house, and toiled long hours without pay. She was sometimes treated harshly by the man who owned her. Most slaves, like Harriet, were not given any schooling, so they did not know how to read or write. Harriet faced a life of few opportunities.

Despite the law, Harriet secretly married John Tubman, a free black man, around 1844. She set her sights on escaping to the North, where slavery was outlawed. Any slave who escaped could be hunted down and sent back into slavery. That is why many slaves wanted to reach Canada—a place that did not recognize the slave laws of the U.S.

Leading Slaves to Freedom

Harriet knew the huge risk she was taking, but she still decided to leave. John did not support her, so she left without him. A white neighbor gave Harriet the name of a "conductor" on the Underground Railroad.

> "I had crossed the line. I was free; but there was no one to welcome me to the land of freedom. I was a stranger in a strange land."
> —Harriet Tubman

The Underground Railroad was not a railroad nor was it under the ground. It was a secret and illegal network of people who helped slaves escape to freedom. These people hid slaves, fed them, and told them where to go next.

The people involved in the Underground Railroad could be arrested or killed if they were discovered. To keep their plans secret, they talked about it in railroad terms. A guide, called a conductor, led slaves to safe houses, called stations. They walked and traveled by boat, horse, wagon, or train—mostly at night.

Harriet Tubman reached safety in Philadelphia,

There were many routes via the Underground Railroad. None would have been possible, though, without the help of brave conductors.

Harriet Tubman

Pennsylvania. However, she felt the urge to go back to Maryland—not as a slave, but as a conductor—to lead other slaves to freedom. She returned to Maryland to help her parents and other family members escape. In all, she made 19 trips to the South to help slaves use the Underground Railroad. She helped about 300 slaves reach freedom and begin new lives.

People called Tubman "Moses," after the man in Biblical times who led the Hebrews out of slavery in Egypt. Slave hunters were aware of the new "Moses" who was helping slaves escape, and they put out a reward for Tubman's capture. However, they thought she was a man! They did not believe that a woman was capable of such dangerous activities. Tubman was never caught.

During the Civil War, which helped end slavery in America, Harriet worked for the Union Army. Not

---

TOPICAL TIDBIT

"Follow the Drinking Gourd"

Slaves used songs to help them travel to safety in the North. One song was "Follow the Drinking Gourd." It contained code words to guide the way. The "drinking gourd" was the Big Dipper in the night sky. By following the gourd, they would find the "promised land" of Canada.

only was she a cook and a nurse, but a spy and scout, too. She helped slaves seek safety with the Union Army.

Courage and Compassion

After the war, Tubman continued to devote her life to others. She started a home for orphaned children and the elderly in Auburn, New York. She died on March 10, 1913, in Auburn.

Rising above her status as a slave in the South, Tubman showed that one woman could change the fate of many others. Her contributions have been honored in many ways, including statues, paintings, and, in 1973, induction into the National Women's Hall of Fame. Harriet's former home in Auburn, New York, is open for tours, allowing people to see how the "Moses of her people" lived.

LIFE EVENTS

1820
Araminta Greene is born in Dorchester County, Maryland.

1849
Tubman escapes to Pennsylvania alone.

1850s
Tubman is a conductor on the Underground Railroad.

1863
The Emancipation Proclamation is signed, freeing slaves in Confederate states.

1908
Tubman opens the Harriet Tubman Home for Aged and Indigent [poor] Colored People.

1913
Harriet Tubman dies in Auburn, New York.

Mary Edwards Walker
Army Doctor
(born 1832 • died 1919)

Only recently have women been accepted into the armed forces and given the same opportunities as men. During the Civil War, however, Mary Edwards Walker served on battlefields and became the only woman ever to earn a Congressional Medal of Honor.

Strong Opinions

Mary Edwards Walker was born in Oswego, New York, on November 26, 1832. Her father was a doctor who believed strongly in education and equality for women. Following his example, Mary grew up believing in women's rights. She also became a follower of Amelia Bloomer, who called for more comfortable and practical clothes for women. As an adult, Mary Edwards Walker followed Bloomer's example of wearing loose-fitting pants (which became known as "bloomers") instead of the tight-fitting, bulky, and uncomfortable dresses women were expected to wear.

In 1855, Walker graduated from Syracuse Medical College. She was the only woman in her class and only the second woman to graduate from a U.S. medical school. The following year, she married another doctor, Albert Miller. Walker broke with tradition by keeping her own name instead of taking her husband's. The couple set up a medical practice together, but the business failed because most people would not accept a female doctor. Walker and Miller separated several years later, and were divorced in 1869.

On the Battlefield

In 1861, the U.S. Civil War broke out between the North and South. Walker traveled to Washington, D.C., and tried to join the Union Army. When she was refused a commission as a medical officer, Walker volunteered as an acting assistant surgeon at the U.S. Patent Office Hospital in Washington. She was the first female surgeon in the United States Army.

In 1863, General George H. Thomas appointed Walker assistant surgeon in the Army of the Cumberland. This finally placed her on the battlefield. Walker served near the front lines for almost two years. She cared for hundreds of sick, injured, and dying soldiers, despite shortages of medicines and supplies. She also served as a spy, and crossed Confederate lines to treat civilians.

> "Dr. Mary lost the medal simply because she was a hundred years ahead of her time."
>
> —a relative of Mary Edwards Walker, to *The New York Times*

Walker was captured by Confederate forces in 1864. She spent four months in a prison in Richmond, Virginia, before being exchanged for a Confederate officer held prisoner by the Union army. Between her release and the war's end in April 1865, Walker worked at a prison for women in Louisville, Kentucky.

The Medal of Honor

On November 11, 1865, President Andrew Johnson awarded the Congressional Medal of Honor to Walker for her contributions to the war effort. She was the only woman to ever receive the Medal,

---

TOPICAL TIDBIT

Walt Whitman

One of the most famous volunteers of the Civil War is also one of America's greatest poets—Walt Whitman. When his brother George was wounded in the Battle of Fredericksburg, Virginia, in December 1862, Whitman rushed from his home in Brooklyn, New York, to the field hospital. After George recovered, Whitman took a job in nearby Washington, D.C. In his spare time, he volunteered his services to the wounded soldiers in the Army hospital. He read to the men, wrote letters for them, and spent what little money he had on small comforts for them. The poet stayed in Washington through the end of the war.

Mary Edwards Walker

which is the country's highest military award.

After the war ended, Walker was elected president of the National Dress Reform Association, a group that campaigned for more comfortable and sensible clothes for women. She often dressed as a man, including a top hat, bow tie, and long coat. Several times, she was arrested for masquerading as a man, a charge that she found ridiculous.

Meanwhile, Walker's war work was publicized by several women's rights organizations, making her a hero to feminists. Walker worked for a variety of social reforms, including the campaign for women's right to vote. Walker attended political meetings and conventions, although she wasn't always allowed to speak. She also wrote several books.

In 1917, Walker received stunning news. Congress had changed the rules for award-

LIFE EVENTS

1832
Mary Edwards Walker is born in Oswego, New York.

1855
Walker graduates from Syracuse Medical College—the second woman to graduate from a U.S. medical school.

1861
The Civil War begins. Walker volunteers and becomes the first female surgeon in the U.S. Army.

1864
Confederate forces capture Walker and hold her prisoner for four months.

1865
Walker is awarded the Congressional Medal of Honor.

1871
Walker publishes the autobiographical book *Hit*.
She dies in 1919.

ing the Medal of Honor and would now recognize only people who had been in "actual combat with an enemy." Walker, along with 910 other people, was asked to return her medal. She refused to return hers, and continued to wear it every day until her death. In 1977, President Jimmy Carter reinstated Walker's medal, citing her "self-sacrifice, patriotism, dedication, and unflinching loyalty to her country, despite the apparent discrimination because of her sex."

Dr. Mary Edwards Walker died in Oswego, New York, on February 21, 1919—just a few months before women were finally awarded the right to vote. In 1982, the U.S. issued a stamp to honor Walker as the first woman to be awarded the Congressional Medal of Honor.

Ida B. Wells-Barnett
Antilynching Crusader
(born 1862 • died 1931)

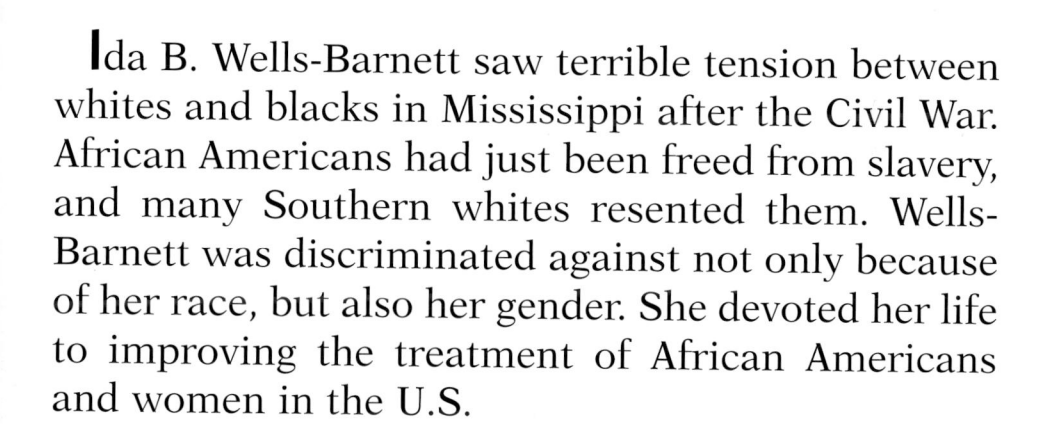

Ida B. Wells-Barnett saw terrible tension between whites and blacks in Mississippi after the Civil War. African Americans had just been freed from slavery, and many Southern whites resented them. Wells-Barnett was discriminated against not only because of her race, but also her gender. She devoted her life to improving the treatment of African Americans and women in the U.S.

Always a Fighter

Ida Bell Wells was born during the Civil War on July 16, 1862, in Holly Springs, Mississippi. She had to be tough. Her parents were slaves who were freed after the war ended in 1865. Times were difficult for blacks in the South as they tried to adjust to life as free men and women. Most slave owners had denied slaves any schooling, so many former slaves could not read or write. It was hard to start businesses or farms on their own because they had little money. They had worked for years as slaves, and received no payment.

Ida had the opportunity to go to school. She was very bright, and became a teacher herself at age 14, after her parents died. In 1884, she went to Tennessee to teach at a country school while attending Fisk University. In Tennessee, Ida experienced prejudice firsthand.

One incident occurred in 1887, when she was thrown off a train for sitting in the whites-only section. The train had separate seating for white passengers and black travelers, but Ida refused to change seats when asked. She sued the railroad because it had not provided equal facilities. She won the case in local court and was awarded $500. Later, however, the Tennessee Supreme Court reversed the decision.

◆ Ida B. Wells-Barnett ◆

A Target of Hate

Ida B. Wells continued to stand up to injustice. She wrote articles about the poor quality of black schools, especially when compared to white schools, which were far superior. Wells lost her teaching job because of these articles so, in 1891, she started a newspaper called the *Memphis Free Speech*. In her articles, she called for an end to discrimination and violence against blacks.

Wells spoke out most passionately against lynching, which was occurring throughout the South. Lynching was when angry mobs of white men hunted African American men and women and dragged them from their homes or jobs. The mobs would beat their victims, then hang them—often for no reason other than the color of their skin. The police, who were white, ignored the murders.

Several of Wells' friends were lynched in the

TOPICAL TIDBIT

The Origins of Lynching

Lynching became popular in the U.S. during the American Revolution, under the direction of Charles Lynch, a planter and patriot from Virginia. He led a group that punished people who remained loyal to Great Britain. The practice became known as *lynching*, and continued for more than 150 years. Between 1882 and 1951, 1,293 whites and 3,437 blacks were lynched in the U.S.

early 1890s. Her newspaper instructed blacks to boycott (refuse to use) white businesses in protest. She became a target herself, and her office was destroyed. Wells was warned to stay away or be killed.

Wells moved to New York and continued her work. In 1895, she married Ferdinand Lee Barnett. Wells kept her maiden name as part of her married name, and became Ida Wells-Barnett. Although this is relatively common today, it was rare, even shocking, in 1895. Also in 1895, Wells-Barnett published a book about lynching called *A Red Record*. Three years later, she went to the White House to urge President William McKinley to take government action to end lynching.

A Nonstop Activist

Wells-Barnett's fight did not end with African American issues. She also fought for women's rights. Wells-Barnett was proof that a woman could be a journalist, activist, wife, and mother of four children. She tried to combine race and gender issues, but some leaders of the women's movement were not very supportive. They feared that adding race to the mix would take away

> "One had better die fighting against injustice than die like a dog or a rat in a trap."
>
> —Ida B. Wells-Barnett

interest and support from the women's movement.

Wells-Barnett started many groups to address social causes, including the Negro Fellowship League and the Alpha Suffrage Club. She was one of the founders of the National Association for the Advancement of Colored People (NAACP) in 1909. The NAACP is an organization that works toward establishing equal rights for African Americans. Wells-Barnett died on March 25, 1931, in Chicago, Illinois.

Ida B. Wells-Barnett described her struggles in her autobiography, *Crusade for Justice*. Although lynching continued in the 20th century, Wells-Barnett fought courageously in the face of death threats. She brought the issue before the eyes of the world and encouraged others to work toward ending injustice.

LIFE EVENTS

1862
Ida Bell Wells is born a slave in Holly Springs, Mississippi.

1887
Wells is forced to sit in third class on a train, even though she had bought a first-class ticket. She sues the train company.

1891
Wells establishes the newspaper *Memphis Free Speech*. She writes articles that call for an end to violence against blacks.

1895
Ida B. Wells marries Ferdinand Lee Barnett and moves to Chicago.

1931
Ida B. Wells-Barnett dies.

Laura Ingalls Wilder
Author
(born 1867 • died 1957)

Laura Ingalls Wilder wrote children's stories about growing up on the prairies of America. Like other pioneers, Wilder's family traveled by covered wagon to places like Nebraska, Minnesota, and North Dakota, hoping to make a new life on the prairie. Wilder's "Little House" books tell of the hardships and joys her family encountered along the way.

Life on the Prairie

Laura Elizabeth Ingalls was born to Charles and Caroline Ingalls on February 7, 1867, in a farmhouse near Pepin, Wisconsin. Laura had four sisters and one brother. Laura and her older sister, Mary, attended the Barry Corner School, learning to read and write. Life was simple but hard. For an evening's entertainment, Charles often played the fiddle while Caroline taught the girls to cook and sew.

When Laura was seven, the family traveled by covered wagon to Walnut Grove, Minnesota, to start a

Laura Ingalls Wilder

farm. When they first arrived, they did not have anyplace to live, so Charles Ingalls built a "dugout" sod house—a hole carved into the side of a hill—on the banks of a creek. Then he built a house of wood. Laura and Mary helped him plant wheat in the fields.

Life on the prairie was often hard. Many times, the crops failed due to droughts or blizzards. In 1874, swarms of grasshoppers invaded the crop fields. Farmers tried to save their crops from the hungry insects by setting fire to straw and manure, hoping that the smoke would kill the grasshoppers. It took two years to rid the land of the jumping insects. In 1879, the Ingalls family moved to De Smet, North Dakota, so Charles could work for the railroad.

Through all the difficulty, Laura continued her studies. She was an excellent student and was interested in literature and history. When Mary was struck by fever and blindness, Laura stayed by her side, helping her with schoolwork and household chores.

Laura worked very hard and received her teaching certificate when she was 15. She took a job as schoolmistress of the Bouchie School, 12 miles from home. Since it was too far to walk each day, she lived with a local family. Laura's friend, Almanzo "Manly"

TOPICAL TIDBIT

Sod Houses

American pioneers traveled west, often settling in the plains where there were few trees. Instead of using lumber to build homes, the pioneers used sod, mud, and clay. They made the roofs from straw and branches. Sometimes, the houses were built into the side of a hill; these were called "dugouts."

Wilder, drove her home each weekend in his horse-drawn wagon, so that she could spend time with her family. In 1885, Laura and Almanzo were married. They lived on a farm near town. The following year, they had a daughter, named Rose.

A Career in Writing

Laura Ingalls Wilder lived in many places over the course of her life. Then, in 1894, she, Manly, and Rose settled in Mansfield, Missouri, in the Ozark Mountains. They built a farm called Rocky Ridge, which remained home. In addition to tending to her home and raising her daughter, Wilder wrote articles for the *Missouri Ruralist* and *McCall's Magazine*. She told Rose about her childhood—about growing up on the prairie and moving from place to place by covered wagon.

> "I am beginning to learn that it is the sweet, simple things in life which are the real ones after all."
>
> —Laura Ingalls Wilder

When Rose was a young woman, she begged her mother to write down those stories of her childhood—about Laura, the young girl who had grown up on the prairie. Rose helped her mother write the stories that were later published as *Little House in the Big Woods*, the first in a series of "Little House" books.

After the success of the first book, Wilder wrote several others, including *Little House on the Prairie, On the Banks of Plum Creek*, and *On the Way Home*. Wilder received the Newbery Award—one of the highest honors given to an author of children's books. In fact, Wilder's books were so popular that, in 1954, the American Library Association created the Laura Ingalls Wilder Award for children's authors. Three years later, on February 10, 1957, Wilder died. She was 90 years old.

Laura Ingalls Wilder captured the hearts of children throughout the world with her "Little House" books. In the 1970s, her stories were turned into a television series called *Little House on the Prairie*. In many places, the shows are still being aired on cable stations.

LIFE EVENTS

1867
Laura Elizabeth Ingalls is born in Lake Pepin, Wisconsin.

1882-1885
Ingalls teaches in the Dakota Territory.

1885
Laura Ingalls marries Almanzo Wilder.

1894
Laura Ingalls Wilder begins writing for the *Missouri Ruralist*.

1935
Wilder writes *Little House on the Prairie*, based on her experiences as part of a pioneer family.

1954
The Laura Ingalls Wilder Award for children's literature is created.

1957
Laura Ingalls Wilder dies.

Oprah Winfrey
Talk-show Host, Actor, Humanitarian
(born 1954)

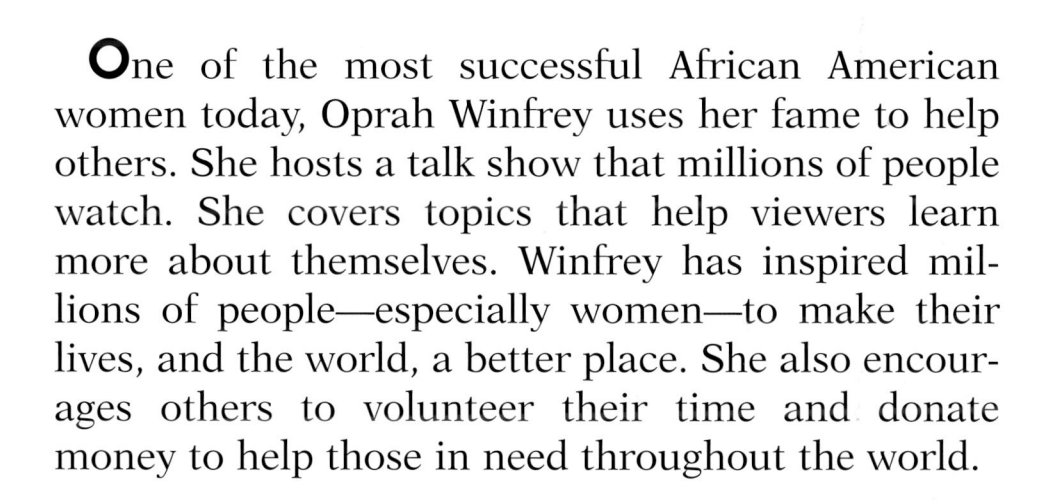

One of the most successful African American women today, Oprah Winfrey uses her fame to help others. She hosts a talk show that millions of people watch. She covers topics that help viewers learn more about themselves. Winfrey has inspired millions of people—especially women—to make their lives, and the world, a better place. She also encourages others to volunteer their time and donate money to help those in need throughout the world.

The "Preacher"

Oprah Winfrey was born January 29, 1954, in Kosciusko, Mississippi. Her parents were unmarried teenagers, and Oprah spent the first six years of

> "Think like a queen. A queen is not afraid to fail. Failure is another stepping-stone to life."
> —Oprah Winfrey

her life with her grandmother. Her parents had given her the biblical name Orpah, but misspelled it.

Winfrey learned to read the Bible when she was about three. At that time, she also began to recite Bible verses and speeches at church. Later, she sometimes repeated sermons at school, so her classmates started to call her "Preacher." Even at such a young age, Winfrey became known for her ability to speak well and captivate an audience.

When Winfrey was six years old, she went to live with her mother in Milwaukee, Wisconsin. There, she was physically abused by several male relatives. Winfrey, who had difficulty dealing with the abuse, often got into trouble and tried to run away. It took years for her to realize that she was not responsible for being abused.

When Winfrey was a teenager, she was sent to Nashville, Tennessee, to live with her father, who was very strict. He set curfews for her and assigned her many book reports, encouraging her love of reading. Winfrey began to settle down and slowly turn her life around.

When she was 19, she began work as a radio reporter. She switched to television reporting while a student at Tennessee State University. In 1977, she took a job as a TV news anchor in Baltimore, Maryland. She remembers trying to act like noted journalist Barbara Walters. However, Winfrey had difficulties as a reporter. She could not remain unaffected by the news stories she read. Sometimes she laughed when a story was funny, or cried when it was sad, which a reporter is not supposed to do. She feared that she would lose her job. Instead, the station assigned her to an early-morning talk show called *People Are Talking*. The format of the show was more casual than reporting the news. Winfrey made the show a success. She believed that she had found her calling in life.

Talking Her Way to the Top

In 1984, Winfrey moved to Chicago to host a talk show called *A.M. Chicago*, which later became the *Oprah Winfrey Show*. In 1986, when the show was broadcast nationwide, Winfrey rose to the top of her profession. By the late 1990s, more than 20 million people were tuning in to see her show every day. Since 1994, Winfrey has vowed to present only helpful or uplifting programs, unlike many other talk shows that present trashy topics.

Eventually, Winfrey started her own production company, Harpo Productions. She took control of the *Oprah Winfrey Show*. She also tried her hand at acting. In 1985, she appeared in Steven Spielberg's film *The Color Purple*. In 1998, she produced and starred in *Beloved*, a film based on a Pulitzer Prize-winning novel by Toni Morrison. She also served as executive producer for television movies, including *Tuesdays with Morrie* (1999) and *Their Eyes Were Watching God* (2005). In 2002, Winfrey's production company launched a talk show starring popular psychologist Dr. Phil McGraw. The show is simply titled *Dr. Phil*.

TOPICAL TIDBIT

Oprah's Book Club

Oprah Winfrey encourages people to read by sponsoring a book club. She gives her television audience time to read each book. Then she arranges for a few viewers to meet the author to discuss the work. Winfrey has recommended books by many writers including Maya Angelou and Toni Morrison.

Oprah Winfrey

Winfrey has won Emmy Awards for television and a Peabody Award, which honors achievement in broadcasting and cable. *Time* magazine named her one of the most influential people of the 20th century.

Winfrey's success has made her one of the richest women in America. However, she strongly believes that people should give back to their communities, so she makes large contributions to charity and works to bring important issues into the public eye. Winfrey worked to get Congress to pass the National Child Protection Act to help abused children. The bill became law in 1993.

In 1998, Winfrey started Oprah's Angel Network. Many viewers of her talk show have contributed to the fund, which is used to help various nonprofit organizations worldwide. She also established the

LIFE EVENTS

1954
Oprah Winfrey is born in Kosciusko, Mississippi.

1984
Winfrey hosts *A.M. Chicago*, which becomes *The Oprah Winfrey Show*.

1985
Winfrey is nominated for an Academy Award for Best Supporting Actress for the movie *The Color Purple*.

1998
Oprah begins Oprah's Angel Network.

2000
Winfrey launches *O: The Oprah Magazine*.

2005
Winfrey receives the National Freedom Award from the National Civil Rights Museum.

Oprah Winfrey Foundation, which works to increase educational opportunities to those in need. Winfrey's charities also help children in South Africa by providing books, clothing, and other necessities. As of 2006, plans are underway to build the Oprah Winfrey Leadership Academy for Girls in South Africa.

Winfrey has also created two magazines: *O, The Oprah Magazine* and *O at Home*. A collection of her memorable talk show moments, marking her 20th anniversary on the air, was released in 2005.

Making a Difference

Oprah Winfrey brings important issues to light, especially problems faced by African Americans, women, and children. Winfrey's abilities to relate to the experiences of her guests and share her own personal stories have allowed her to help many people improve their lives. Her charitable work improves the lives of many people throughout the world.

Babe Didrikson Zaharias
Athlete
(born 1911 • died 1956)

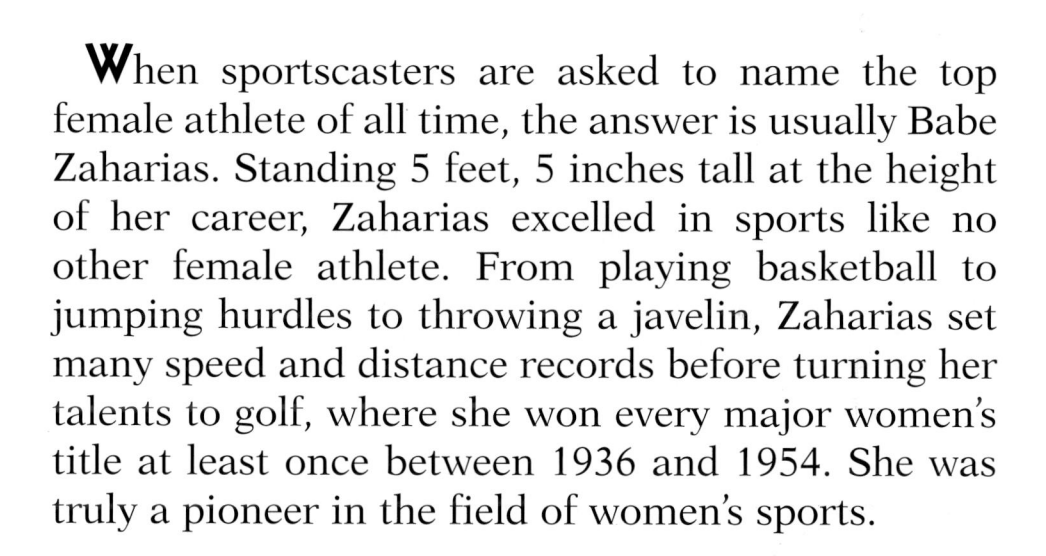

When sportscasters are asked to name the top female athlete of all time, the answer is usually Babe Zaharias. Standing 5 feet, 5 inches tall at the height of her career, Zaharias excelled in sports like no other female athlete. From playing basketball to jumping hurdles to throwing a javelin, Zaharias set many speed and distance records before turning her talents to golf, where she won every major women's title at least once between 1936 and 1954. She was truly a pioneer in the field of women's sports.

Becoming an Athlete

Mildred Ella Didrikson was born on June 26, 1911, in Port Arthur, Texas. After a hurricane flattened the city in 1914, her family moved to Beaumont, 17 miles inland from the sea.

As a young girl, Mildred loved all types of sports,

◇ 50 American Women ◇

Babe Didrikson boxes to keep in shape (1933).

including swimming, diving, tennis, bowling, football, cycling, figure skating, handball, and volleyball. After hitting five home runs during a school baseball game, her classmates started calling her "Babe," after Babe Ruth. Babe's parents were very supportive of her athletic abilities. They encouraged her to try out for the basketball team. She played on the All-American girls' basketball team from 1930 to 1932.

Heading for the Olympics

On July 16, 1932, Didrikson competed at the Olympic trials in Evanston, Illinois. She competed in 10 track-and-field events and won 8. By the end of the day, Didrikson was a member of the U.S. Olympic Team.

The 1932 Olympics were held in Los Angeles, California. Didrikson qualified for five events, but because she was a woman, she was only allowed to compete in three. She set world records for the javelin toss (143 feet, 4 inches) and the 80-meter hurdles (11.7 seconds). She also broke the world record for the high jump but was disqualified because her head went over the bar before the rest of her body. (This is known as the "Western Roll" and is now acceptable in high-jump competition.) Didrikson won two gold medals (for

> "Before I was even in my teens, I knew exactly what I wanted to be when I grew up. My goal was to be the greatest athlete who ever lived."
>
> —Babe Didrickson Zaharias

the javelin and 80-meter hurdles) and one silver (for the high jump).

The World of Golf

In 1935, Didrikson turned her attention to golf. Believing that practice makes perfect, she would practice for eight hours straight, hitting more than 1,000 golf balls each day. Didrikson could take a swing and hit the ball more than 250 yards, landing it where she wanted it to go.

Didrikson played golf for the next 20 years. In 1946 and 1947 alone, she won 17 out of the 18 tournaments in which she played. In total, she won 41 tournaments, including the U.S. National Women's Amateur Championship (1946) and the British Ladies' Amateur Championship (1947). She also won

---

TOPICAL TIDBIT

Ladies' Professional Golf Association

Babe Didrikson Zaharias was one of the founders of the Ladies' Professional Golf Association (LPGA). The LPGA is now one of the top professional golf organizations in the world. Some of the other founding members were Patty Berg, Helen Dettweiler, Opal Hill, Betty Jameson, and Louise Suggs. Some of today's stars include Nancy Lopez, Se Ri Pak, and Annika Sorenstam.

Babe Didrikson Zaharias tees off at the Women's British Amateur Championship in Scotland, 1947.

the U.S. Women's Open three times—in 1948, 1950, and 1954. She was one of the founders of the Ladies' Professional Golf Association (LPGA).

In 1938, Didrikson met George Zaharias when they were paired at a golf tournament. Zaharias was a pro wrestler called the "Weeping Greek from Cripple

Creek." They were married later that year. George became Babe's manager.

Gone too Soon

In 1953, Babe Zaharias was diagnosed with cancer. She had surgery in 1953 and again in 1956, but the cancer spread quickly. Babe died of cancer on September 27, 1956, in Galveston, Texas. She was only 42.

Babe Didrikson Zaharias has earned as many honors in death as she did in life. The Associated Press named her Woman Athlete of the Year many times. *Sport's Illustrated* magazine called her the Female Athlete of the Century in 1999. She has also been memorialized in other ways—the Babe Didrikson Zaharias Memorial Center in Beaumont, Texas, is a museum dedicated to her career in sports. The Babe Zaharias Foundation raises money for cancer research.

LIFE EVENTS

1914
Mildred Ella Didrikson is born in Port Arthur, Texas.

1931
At the National Women's Amateur Athletic Union (AAU) track meet, Didrikson wins first place in eight events.

1932
Didrikson breaks three world records in track and field events at the Olympics.

1950
Babe Didrikson Zaharias is named Athlete of the Half Century by the Associated Press.

1954
Zaharias wins the U.S. Women's Open in golf for the third time.

1956
Zaharias dies of cancer.